"Through education, reassurance, validation, and exercises that raise awaren̶.̶.̶ ̶a̶n̶d̶ ̶t̶e̶a̶c̶h̶ ̶p̶o̶w̶e̶r̶f̶u̶l̶ ̶s̶k̶i̶l̶l̶s̶, *Hope and Healing for Survivors* offers survivors concrete guidance and hope. Stacey Pinatelli's workbook is grounded, compassionate, and empowering."

    —**Matthew Cordova, PhD**, clinical psychologist, and professor at Palo Alto University

"As a trauma therapist who has worked with survivors for over sixteen years, I highly recommend this workbook. Whether using alone or as an adjunct to therapy, Pinatelli gently leads readers through the healing process with empathy and compassion. Through psychoeducation and practical exercises, her workbook helps individuals build their capacity to process trauma, and empowers them to create the life they envision."

    —**Kate Stanford, LMHC, CCTP-II**, trauma-focused therapist at the UR Medicine HEAL Collaborative in Rochester, NY, working with adults recovering from interpersonal violence

"*Hope and Healing for Survivors* offers female survivors of childhood sexual abuse not only a much-needed sense of hope, but also a beautifully structured opportunity to process their trauma-related experiences. Pinatelli thoughtfully integrates clinical knowledge and heartfelt emotion throughout this powerful workbook. Each chapter, activity, checkpoint, and reflection utilize personal and reader-friendly language that allows survivors to progress at their own pace and manage feelings of overwhelm on their way to resiliency."

    —**Hadas Pade, PsyD**, licensed clinical psychologist in Northern California who has worked in community mental health and academia for nearly twenty years, and currently teaches and supervises at The Wright Institute in Berkeley, CA

"Written with an authentic voice and accessible language, Pinatelli captures with clarity the stages of healing from childhood sexual abuse. Grounded in easy-to-understand conceptual explanations, the clear and focused exercises that Pinatelli has created lead the reader from awareness, through acceptance, self-care, and insight for integration of a balanced self-narrative—that is, from surviving to thriving."

    —**Reverend Christine M. Fahrenbach, PhD**, clinical psychologist, former adjunct faculty at Palo Alto University and John F. Kennedy University, and Roman Catholic Womanpriest

"I work for a hospital at an adult behavioral health center. I found Stacey Pinatelli's book to be a practical and inspirational guide. It provides useful applications of DBT for working with clients who have had traumatic experiences. I thought the book could be used in sessions with clients as an adjunct, or possibly as a stand-alone self-help manual. Thanks for the opportunity to view this material."

> —**John Behling, LCSW, DCSW**, clinical social worker in adult outpatient behavioral health services at Eastern Connecticut Health Network

"*Hope and Healing for Survivors* is a much-needed addition to the field of trauma treatment, especially for those who are not yet ready to let someone else in for this process of (re)building self-compassion, understanding, and acceptance. This workbook is a thoughtful and compassionate guide. It is a glimmer of light in the darkness. It is hope for those who have suffered that healing is in fact possible. Sometimes, that is all we need."

> —**Joanna Fava, PhD**, clinical assistant professor of psychology in psychiatry at Weill Cornell Medicine, and clinician/supervisor/consultant in private practice specializing in treating trauma and its impact

Hope and Healing for Survivors

A Workbook for Women Who Have Experienced Childhood Sexual Abuse

Stacey R. Pinatelli, PsyD

New Harbinger Publications, Inc.

Publisher's Note

NEW HARBINGER PUBLICATIONS is a registered trademark of New Harbinger Publications, Inc.

New Harbinger Publications is an employee-owned company.

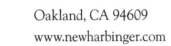

Copyright © 2024 by Stacey R. Pinatelli
New Harbinger Publications, Inc.
5720 Shattuck Avenue
Oakland, CA 94609
www.newharbinger.com

Cover design by Amy Shoup

Acquired by Jennye Garibaldi

Edited by Marisa Solis

Printed in the United States of America

26   25   24

10   9   8   7   6   5   4   3   2   1   First Printing

To my husband, Tommy Pinatelli, for honoring the resilient and strong-willed woman I am for the last thirty-four years. In honor of my mom, who taught me more about resilience than any textbook and encouraged me to pursue my passion for helping other survivors. Although you were unable to witness the completion of this project, you remain in my heart. I am grateful to my dad, who has continuously supported me throughout my life and always been my voice of reason when my trauma voice sought to steer me in a different direction.

Contents

Foreword

"Although the world is full of suffering, it is also full of the overcoming of it."

—Helen Keller

After nearly 30 years of helping survivors heal from their trauma, I am still struck by both the level of suffering and the incredible healing that can occur following long-standing exposure to traumatic events. I have worked with clients in psychotherapy who have suffered years-long sexual abuse at the hands of a parent or sibling and clients who have encountered unspeakable acts of violence and emotional brutality inside what is supposed to be a safe and loving system of care. Hearing the stories of these victims has, at times, skewed my understanding of humanity, falling into great skepticism about our ability to extend kindness and love, especially to those who are most vulnerable. However, the very victims themselves continually restore my faith in humankind as I see those wounded by extensive trauma histories bloom into living meaningful lives that are no longer defined by their pasts.

The stories of these victims and the lasting impact of their experiences are often referred to as *complex trauma*, with exposure to trauma frequently beginning in childhood and lasting for years. Additionally, these traumatic experiences typically involved close interpersonal relationships, such as those found in families, extended family, and other close connections. Unlike single-incident traumas such as accidents or natural disasters, complex trauma involves repeated or chronic exposure to stressors such as physical or emotional abuse, neglect, or violence, with these stressors leading to profound and lasting effects on an individual's psychological, emotional, and social development.

The impact is significant, with the suffering, distress, and sorrow palpable. I have found myself, at times, quite angry at those who cause such grief—again, renewed to letting go and moving on at witnessing the resiliency of the survivor.

The possibility of change and resiliency brings me to this book: *Hope and Healing for Survivors: A Workbook for Women Who Have Experienced Childhood Sexual Abuse*. Given that this type of past can disrupt a person's sense of safety, trust, attachment, and understanding of the self and the world, leading to difficulties in forming healthy relationships that are defined by healthy intimacy and boundaries, and that it can lead to an understanding of self contaminated with unwanted and undeserved messages of faultiness and fear, *Hope and Healing for Survivors* lends just the right self-help work to begin the journey of healing.

Treatment for complex trauma often involves a comprehensive approach that addresses the underlying traumatic experiences, helping individuals to develop coping skills, and supporting them in building healthy relationships and a sense of safety and stability. *Hope and Healing for Survivors* provides the information needed to understand why survivors think the way they do while connecting them to tools that promote safety and trust. The book comprehensively guides the survivor through a self-reflective process designed to lift the survivor out of the past and into a healthy future. Working on schemas, healthy coping, compassion, self-acceptance, and mindfulness, author Stacey R. Pinatelli, a survivor herself, has created a guide to assist those knocked down by trauma to find the courage, strength, and skills to stand again. The exercises and rhythm of the book are well-timed, allowing the survivor the grace and self-pacing to explore recovery and begin to trust again.

It is my belief, deep hope, and heart-felt wish that those exploring *Hope and Healing for Survivors* will find their way back to a sense of self that is stable and thoughtfully able to move forward in life with a sense of direction, purpose, and values-guided action. Stacey Pinatelli has created just the right exploratory process and guidance to assist those reading and doing the work in blooming into a life of meaning, no longer chained to a painful past and the effects of long-standing trauma. Helen Keller said it well: There is suffering, but there is also the overcoming of suffering. There is hope and healing.

—Robyn D. Walser, PhD

Introduction

My desire to create this workbook grew out of my own experience as a childhood sexual abuse survivor. As a child, I was not able to access psychotherapy, nor did I feel supported within my family to discuss the complex feelings and thoughts I had about myself at the time. As a result, I learned how to suppress and avoid those feelings. After working for quite some time, this coping strategy suddenly ceased to function, leaving me even more confused than before. By acknowledging my suppressed feelings, I developed trust in myself and others, helpful coping skills, and, eventually, hope. My healing journey and the value of my own resilience began with this moment.

The road to self-acceptance was not linear, and I made mistakes along the way. In spite of the fact that the path to hope and resilience can be frightening and rocky, I can say with confidence that I have grown into the person I am today as a result of learning how to accept and experience pain. With an emphasis on trauma-focused treatments, I am dedicated to a career in clinical psychology so that I may assist survivors like myself in learning how to live beyond the pain. In developing this workbook, I've been motivated by my passion to aid survivors such as yourself on their journey to healing and resilience.

You may be able to relate to my experiences as you read this. You may, however, find it difficult to acknowledge your own feelings and thoughts. This is understandable, and you are not alone. While you already possess all the elements necessary for healing, it's important to acknowledge that much of what you've experienced and felt since the sexual abuse has been directly related to it. If you have self-critical thoughts, you may be unable to treat yourself with the compassion you deserve, and you may find it difficult to nurture yourself in the way you should.

The most important thing you need to know when you feel shame, sadness, fear, or confusion is that there is another way to cope with these feelings. The first step may be to simply have the hope that you will be able to recover. It may be that you chose this workbook today because you desire to heal yourself. Your inner voice may be telling you that you have the capacity to heal, and that is why you've chosen this exact moment in time to pick up this workbook. You may know you can heal but need support and encouragement to regain confidence in yourself. The fact is, when you were abused, you were not in control. Now, you are in control of your healing process.

My wish is that this workbook will offer the glimmer of hope you need to keep pushing toward what I already know you can do: not just survive but thrive and ultimately inspire others. By gaining an awareness of who you are, as well as skills that will allow you to get to know yourself better, you'll be better able to accept yourself just as you are.

When you acknowledge the root of your suffering, who you are, and what you value in life, you can begin nurturing and loving yourself in a more compassionate way. As you work your way through this book, I hope you'll sense that I'm holding hope for you as you develop the skills that will lead you to a more meaningful life based on your values and strengths.

How This Workbook Can Help You

Chapters 1 through 3 provide an opportunity to examine your perspective on yourself and others, as well as your reactions to certain situations. By increasing your self-awareness first, you'll become more aware of the feelings and thoughts that may have been avoided in the past. Unless you understand why you say or do certain things to cope with trauma, it's difficult to accept yourself. You'll be able to explore parts of yourself that you may not have previously considered or even wanted to explore. The exercises will help you become more accepting and learn alternative coping strategies.

From chapters 4 to 5, you'll learn how nurturing yourself and practicing self-compassion can enhance your hope to heal. The exercises presented in these chapters will help you evaluate your values, accomplishments, and aspects that you enjoy about yourself. In doing so, you'll increase your sense of self-acceptance and ensure that your actions align with your values to live the life you desire.

In the final chapter, mindfulness plays a significant role. By learning to practice mindfulness, you can practice coping strategies that alter how your brain reacts to stress and painful memories.

Doing the Exercises

Some of the exercises in this workbook will focus on what you think about yourself and others, and other exercises will ask you to examine your reactions to certain situations. The exercises will vary, but all of them are designed to help you explore your inner feelings and thoughts. Often, you will explore your feelings through writing, while other times you'll do so by practicing a mindfulness technique and recording your reactions. Certain activities can be completed in one sitting, and other activities will require you to do them over a few weeks.

Each section starts with a psychoeducation piece to allow you to broaden your understanding of the possible effects sexual abuse might have played in your life. There's also an overview of how developing coping strategies can help mitigate those effects. Each section will end with a summary called Tying It All Together, which will allow you to reflect on your feelings, thoughts, and anything you may have learned about yourself or sexual abuse in general.

This workbook is intended to be used in the order it's presented to allow each stage of healing to build upon one another, starting with building a strong sense of self. However, feel free to skip around and complete it in any order that seems right for you. It's more important for you to pick activities that meet your current need rather than trying to complete the workbook in a certain order.

You may find that on some days you're unable to concentrate, or you may feel too triggered by an exercise to complete it. That is okay. Listen to your mind and body. If you encounter an exercise that you're not ready to do, skip it. Come back to it when you're ready. By choosing activities that fit your current need or mood on a certain day, you're practicing self-care, allowing yourself to listen to your inner voice, and taking control of your healing process.

COPING WITH UNCOMFORTABLE THOUGHTS AND FEELINGS

Before you begin the process of self-reflection, it's important to understand that this workbook may bring about uncomfortable sensations. During this process you may experience some of the following:

- Intense thoughts and feelings

- Memories or flashbacks

- Dissociation

With *dissociation*, you may feel as if you're disconnected from your body or the world around you. If this happens, try standing up, holding an ice cube, or tapping your feet on the ground. These techniques can bring you back to the present.

Throughout this workbook, you should practice checking in with yourself to assess whether you are emotionally able or even desire to continue with a specific task. It is natural to feel some level of anxiousness and discomfort when thinking about traumatic events, but if you suddenly feel sensations of panic or intense emotions—such as rage, fear, or hopelessness—this may be a good indication you need to stop the exercise immediately.

You can practice self-care by acknowledging that what you're feeling is part of the healing process. By practicing acceptance and allowing yourself to be okay with where you are and what you're feeling, you provide yourself with the nurturing you may or may not have received after the sexual abuse occurred.

If you experience overwhelming feelings or thoughts that do not subside after you've stopped an exercise, it might be helpful to reach out to someone on your Support System List (at the end of the Introduction). You don't need to be alone through your healing process. Contact a support person as often as you need while you complete these exercises.

CHECK-IN POINTS

Throughout this workbook you'll encounter check-in points designed to remind you to stop, think, reflect, and assess your feelings. These are your cues to gauge whether you would like to continue, practice a grounding technique from chapter 6, or take a break. The check-in points will look like this:

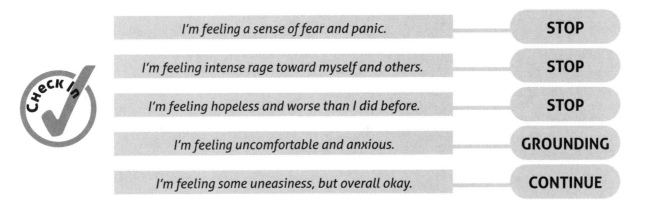

I'm feeling a sense of fear and panic. — **STOP**

I'm feeling intense rage toward myself and others. — **STOP**

I'm feeling hopeless and worse than I did before. — **STOP**

I'm feeling uncomfortable and anxious. — **GROUNDING**

I'm feeling some uneasiness, but overall okay. — **CONTINUE**

When you come to this junction in the workbook, inhale deeply and fully exhale your breath. Then ask yourself the questions in the box.

If you need to stop, use the following sequence to determine your next steps:

- Notice the emotion or sensation that you're feeling in your body.

- If you need to ground yourself, choose a grounding technique from chapter 6, such as:
  - Deep breathing
  - Reaching out to someone on your Support System List
  - Journaling
  - Seeking the counsel of a psychotherapist

> This workbook is not intended to take the place of professional help. During the course of using this workbook, if you feel hopeless or worse than you did before, it is recommended that you stop and consider contacting a mental health professional for further evaluation.

About Word Choice

Certain terms are used intentionally throughout this workbook:

Survivor: Refers to those who were sexually abused as children. The term "survivor" portrays a sense of control, strength, and a more positive way of projecting the process that occurs with abuse. Surviving began when you got through the traumatic event and learned to cope and adapt. As you gain hope and resilience, you may begin to feel as though your survival of trauma can now help you establish a new identity as a survivor, even if you are not yet aware that you are one.

Healing process: The process those that have been abused go through. It is based on three relevant theories regarding childhood sexual abuse: the childhood sexual abuse (CSA) healing model, attachment theory, and family systems theory.

- **The childhood sexual abuse (CSA) healing model**: Describes the long-term effects of sexual abuse and the different stages survivors go through after abuse. Draucker et al. (2011) describe four stages of healing: *grappling with the meaning of CSA*, *figuring out the meaning of CSA*, *tackling the effects of CSA*, and *laying claim to one's life*.

  When you *grapple with the meaning of CSA*, you may have difficulty understanding how the abuse has impacted your current life, or you may experience significant self-blame.

  Once you've determined that childhood sexual abuse was abusive regardless of the circumstances (for example, age at the time of abuse or response to the abuse), and you're convinced that you were not at fault, you may be in the stage of *figuring out the meaning of CSA*.

  You may be in the *tackling the effects of CSA* stage if you've ended toxic relationships, improved your physical health, and sought out educational or occupational opportunities.

  When you reach the point of *laying claim to one's life* stage, you'll believe that overcoming the effects of childhood sexual abuse has enabled you to decide how you want your life to progress in the future. As a result, you'll feel empowered to live a fulfilling and meaningful life.

  While you go through the healing process, these stages can be painful at times. Yet, as you move through them, you'll begin to feel hopeful, and an inner drive to survive will surface. That is when you'll know you're becoming resilient and the effects of the abuse you may have experienced are manageable. You may be in the process of identifying your trauma voice, making the decision to heal, recognizing that the abuse is not your fault, coping with residual feelings and thoughts, talking about what happened and how it may have affected your life now, or moving forward.

  Regardless of which stage of healing you are in, accepting where you are in the process is the first step toward hope and developing coping strategies that will help guide you along your path toward healing.

- **Attachment theory**: Attachment bonds are necessary for survival. The bonds we form with parental figures in childhood influence our ability to feel safe and supported in future relationships (Bowlby 1973). For instance, if you did not feel attached, safe, or supported by a parental figure or caregiver, you may now find it difficult to make or maintain affectional bonds.

- **Family systems theory**: The behaviors of family members can affect the healing process for a survivor, especially if sexual abuse occurred within the family, because it damages a survivor's ability to trust and interact with others (Karakurt and Silver 2014).

Support system: Refers to anyone to whom you currently can turn for comfort, compassion, and support. This may be an intimate partner, a friend, a parent, a sibling, or a therapist. It may be helpful to join a support group for survivors if you don't feel you have anyone you can turn to and you're not actively seeking therapy. Additionally, you might consider joining a group in your community that provides you with pleasure or happiness, such as a spiritual group.

The Importance of Establishing a Support System

Establishing a support system is vital to the healing process. You may become overwhelmed or stuck as you work through painful feelings and thoughts, and a support system can offer you the compassion and nurturing that you need. Establishing a social network can help reduce feelings of loneliness and hopelessness that may occur during the healing process.

In order to establish a support system, you'll need to assess the relationships in your life that bring you the greatest feelings of trust and compassion. As a survivor, it may be difficult to distinguish which relationships are truly supportive, especially if as a child you grew up in an environment where those closest to you were the ones who hurt or abused you. This list will help you decide which people are best suited to support you. Once you've determined your support system, refer to this list any time you need assistance.

Support System List

Write down the names of all the people you interact with on a continuous basis. Include friends, colleagues, family members, neighbors, community group members, people from support groups that you're involved in, and mental health professionals that you may be seeing. Even if you're not sure you can rely on or confide in certain people, list them anyway.

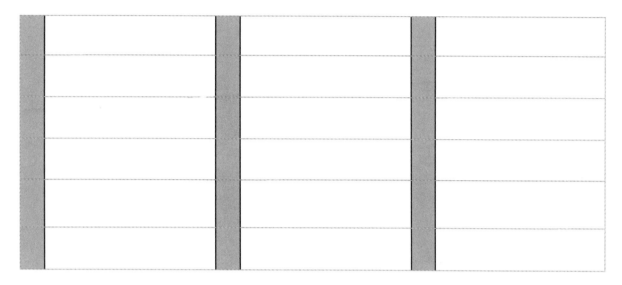

Next, place a checkmark (✓) next to the names of people who have been supportive to you in the past and whom you feel you can trust. Circle the names of people who know you are a survivor. Place an asterisk (*) next to the people who know you are a survivor *and* who have constantly supported you through your healing process. Cross out the names of those who are not supportive—those who ridicule your experience or criticize you.

Now, review your list and notice the names with an asterisk. These people are likely the handful who have consistently been part of your support system, have demonstrated a willingness to show up when you needed them, and offered words of wisdom that helped you feel better. List three to five of these people below. These are your go-tos. Although you might seek support from many or all the people with asterisks or checkmarks, it can be helpful to identify a close few to whom you can turn in crisis or emotional distress.

1. _____

2. _____

3. _____

4. _____

5. _____

CHAPTER 1

The Healing Journey: Understanding Yourself

"Owning our story can be hard but not nearly as difficult as spending our lives running from it."

—Brené Brown

Understanding yourself begins by becoming aware of how past abuse has shaped the way you think, feel, and behave. Thoughts can direct emotions, and in order to manage these emotions, you must first be aware of them. This chapter will help you explore the effects of the childhood sexual abuse you experienced. Understanding how abuse impacted you will allow you to accept where you are in the healing process and learn to stay present in the present moment, which will help you when triggers or distressing events occur.

You may find it difficult to stay in the present moment. You may often spend time thinking about the past or future. By becoming aware of your thoughts, emotions, and bodily sensations, you can tap into how you feel in the present moment. The way you perceive yourself and the world around you is most likely a direct result of your experience of childhood sexual abuse. Once you become aware and understand how you may have been impacted by the abuse, you'll be able to learn how to accept where you are and maintain a sense of grounding. You'll be introduced to grounding techniques in chapter 6.

Trauma Responses, Memories, and Disclosure

Considering how you responded at the time of the abuse and how you react today to reminders of the abuse will give you a deeper understanding of how the abuse has impacted you. You'll be able to identify helpful and unhelpful coping strategies. Abused children often find a way to live through abuse and cope with the aftermath of these experiences. You may have experienced one or more of these common trauma responses:

Fight: The act of confronting a threat typically in an angry verbal or physical manner.

Flight: An attempt to flee from a perceived threat that may manifest as feeling anxious, avoiding a perceived threat, or repressing memories of abuse

Freeze: Shutting down in order to block out the threat, also expressed through dissociation or a feeling of numbness

Fawn: The tendency to appease threats that may manifest as people-pleasing or an inability to set boundaries

These responses are often a necessary and effective coping mechanism for an abused child's survival. When you are confronted with memories of the abuse or with situations that feel emotionally or physically harmful, you may have reverted to these common responses. In adulthood, if intrusive memories of abuse recur, you may continue to respond by engaging in one of the above trauma responses (which we'll discuss more in chapter 3).

Disclosing the abuse can be a painful experience that brings up feelings of shame, guilt, and anger. You may have been supported when you disclosed your abuse, or you may have felt unsupported, blamed for the abuse, or not believed. An unsupported experience can affect your ability to confide in others, reach out for support, and alter how you see yourself (MacGinley, Breckenridge, and Mowell 2019; Taylor and Norma 2013).

Where Are You Right Now?

To assess where you are currently, check off all that apply to you:

☐ I have vivid memories of the abuse that often interrupt my ability to complete daily activities.

☐ Although I don't recall the abuse clearly, I feel that it occurred.

☐ I have fragmented memories of being sexually abused, but I'm unsure who did it.

☐ I know who abused me and I remember the events clearly.

☐ I've avoided thinking about the abuse, but I'm beginning to think that, despite my attempt to push these memories away, it has impacted me.

☐ I've never told anyone about the sexual abuse because I felt ashamed and thought I wouldn't be believed.

☐ I blame myself for what happened.

☐ When I disclosed the sexual abuse, I was believed and felt supported.

☐ The reaction I received when I disclosed the abuse was unsupportive and negative, and I refrained from telling anyone else.

I'm feeling a sense of fear and panic.	**STOP**
I'm feeling intense rage toward myself and others.	**STOP**
I'm feeling hopeless and worse than I did before.	**STOP**
I'm feeling uncomfortable and anxious.	**GROUNDING**
I'm feeling some uneasiness, but overall okay.	**CONTINUE**

CHECK IN ✓

Somatic and Sensory Memories

Whether you remember the abuse fully or not, memories or even a feeling that something happened can influence how you may view yourself and interact with others. Traumatic experiences leave behind more than just mental images. The physical sensations and emotional reactions triggered by these memories can have a profound impact on your body, your memory, and the functioning of your brain.

A *somatic memory* refers to a memory associated with the body and is usually felt in some part of the body. Perhaps you're unaware that certain sensations in your body are linked to traumatic memories. Perhaps you still experience pain or discomfort caused by traumatic memories stored in your body that surface in your everyday life. This is known as a *somatic flashback*. During a flashback, it can be extremely frightening to relive the pain and fear you may have experienced as a child. There are many physiological manifestations associated with these somatic memories, including sweating, a racing heartbeat, and sudden pains in nearly any part of the body.

There are survivors who do not experience flashbacks, and there are survivors who are unaware of having experienced flashbacks. Some survivors feel certain sensations in their body but aren't certain they're connected to stored traumatic memories. If you have indeed experienced a somatic memory, it may have felt like you were experiencing what happened during abuse. These moments may even make you feel like you were a young child again. The trauma you experienced may still remain in your mind or in your body even if you have not experienced a flashback. You may also experience somatic changes associated with traumatic memories in response to triggering circumstances, such as sensory stimuli or bodily sensations.

Sensory memories are fragments of visual images, smells, sounds, tastes, or physical touch that are associated with what you experienced during sexual abuse. These memories are stored in the amygdala, the part of the brain that holds the emotional significance of the trauma. For example, if a specific sound, image, or smell feels distressing and brings back memories of the trauma, this may be a sensory memory of the trauma.

If you have trouble recalling certain memories or a particular period of time, your brain may have blocked them out. This is called *dissociative amnesia*, an involuntary reaction to a traumatic event or negative emotions in order to help you cope.

The following exercise will help you practice being aware of how your body and mind may have responded to memories and negative responses to *disclosure*. By linking your memories with any bodily or sensory clues you may have, you can gain useful insight and make connections (Davis 1990). While this exercise may be completed in one sitting, reflection often takes time, so please pace yourself generously.

Focus on a happy memory first, so that you're relaxed while you practice bringing your attention to sensations in your body (somatic memories) and sensory cues (sensory memories). For example, thinking about a time you rode a roller coaster may bring up sensory information of fear, speed, or excitement. When your mind drifts back to this memory, you may recall experiencing a rapid heart rate (somatic memory) or hear the sounds of the roller coaster (sensory memory).

1. To begin, get into a comfortable position and close your eyes for a few minutes.

2. Take a moment to focus on a happy memory and notice what happens in your body as your mind drifts back to it. Observe whether you are experiencing discomfort or not.

3. Then, when you're ready, open your eyes and respond to the writing prompts. Use the examples as a guide and complete it based on your own memories, feelings, and thoughts.

Memories and sensations I feel in my body:

Sexual intimacy often leaves me feeling ashamed or sickened.

During sex, I often cry without knowing why I'm crying.

When my partner touches me, my first response is to cringe.

I feel guilty when I enjoy sex or want to have sex more than my partner does.

_____

_____

_____

_____

_____

Memories and cues I experience based on senses:

When I see someone with facial hair, I instantly try to avoid that person.

Whenever I'm in a crowded room, I look around for exits to ensure my safety.

The smell of perfume or cologne makes me nauseous.

_____

_____

_____

_____

_____

Feelings, events, and periods of time that might be associated with dissociative amnesia (memory loss):

When I was ten years old, I don't remember moving from one place to another.

I don't remember ever feeling like other kids did, and I often felt distant from those my age.

There are gaps in my memory between the ages of nine and eleven.

_____

_____

_____

_____

Telling about the abuse (disclosure):

In order to avoid disrupting my family dynamics, I put the needs of my family above my own safety, so I never disclosed anything to anyone.

When I told my family, they didn't believe me and told me to forget about it.

My family believed me and supported me through the healing process.

_____

_____

_____

_____

_____

Reflect

Take a moment to reflect on your answers. Notice whether any memories led to other memories that you may not have been aware of previously. If you became aware of how certain bodily and sensory memories may be associated with current feelings, describe what being aware of these associations feels like to you now.

_____

_____

_____

_____

_____

_____

On a scale of 1 to 10, rate your level of hope both *before* you began this chapter and *currently.*

    1 = feeling completely hopeless

    10 = feeling extremely hopeful

Before the chapter _____

After the chapter _____

Emotional Avoidance

You are not alone if you've tried to avoid memories, thoughts, feelings, or sensations associated with your traumatic experiences. Survivors of childhood sexual abuse often use avoidance strategies to reduce the pain associated with their memories. *Avoidance* refers to any action intended to prevent the occurrence of an unpleasant emotion, such as fear, sadness, or shame.

There are many different types of avoidant behaviors, including social withdrawal, avoiding triggers of painful memories, and using coping mechanisms such as substance abuse and binge eating, which are often used to avoid emotions. In order to protect yourself and survive childhood sexual abuse, you may have found that escape was the best option for you at the time. In childhood, avoidance coping strategies may have helped you deal with unsafe situations. But now that you're no longer in that environment, those strategies are no longer useful. You may have attempted to avoid feeling pain, anger, powerlessness, loneliness, confusion, shame, disappointment, rejection, or judgment.

You may have suppressed thoughts like, "I don't deserve to be loved," "I am damaged," or "I am not good enough." All of which may have resulted in low self-esteem, lack of confidence, or feeling empty. Nevertheless, you may have attempted to fix how you felt using certain strategies in the hope that these feelings and thoughts would simply disappear.

Unfortunately, a tendency to avoid emotions can lead to more harm than good, since avoidance behaviors are associated with more severe symptoms of post-traumatic stress disorder (PTSD) and a greater likelihood that you'll feel unsafe in the present moment. To effectively deal with distressing emotions, it's helpful for you to understand how and why you may avoid them. As you become aware of avoidant behaviors that you've used in the past or that you might still use, you can learn how to identify alternative coping strategies that may help you recognize the urge to push feelings and thoughts down.

Refer to the Common Avoidant Behaviors chart to identify the strategies you may have used to make difficult feelings or thoughts go away. Place an X in the first box to indicate that you've used this strategy in the past, and place an X in the second box to indicate that you are currently using this strategy.

Common Avoidant Behaviors

Efforts made to reduce emotional distress	Strategy used in the past	Strategy currently using
Burying your emotions		
Using distraction to not think or feel		
Self-medicating with alcohol or drugs		

Efforts made to reduce emotional distress	Strategy used in the past	Strategy currently using
Avoiding places and activities that cause you to reexperience the event		
Isolating from friends, family, or coworkers		
Cutting or other self-injury		
Overeating or not eating enough		
Risk-taking behaviors (driving fast, adrenaline seeking, sexual promiscuity, and so forth)		
Avoiding people, places, things, or activities that feel activating to you		
Telling your mind, "Don't think about these things"		
Always saying yes or staying quiet to please others		
Preparing for what-ifs by playing the details in your mind in the hope of protecting yourself from disappointment		

Reflect

Take a moment to reflect on your answers. The following questions may increase your awareness of the ways you may have attempted to make emotions go away. In the above chart, which strategies have provided you with temporary relief? How long did this relief last? If it didn't last, what happened next?

_____

_____

_____

_____

How would you spend your time if you were not occupied with managing your difficult feelings thoughts, sensations, memories, and urges?

_____

_____

_____

_____

As part of your efforts to resolve this problem, what do you believe you have given up?

_____

_____

_____

Imagine that you could move in the direction of the type of life that you most desire to lead. How would that look?

_____

_____

_____

_____

To determine the true cost of being caught in the struggle of managing your emotions, take a moment to recall a recent situation in which you experienced negative thoughts or emotions. How did you respond to this experience and what were the costs or consequences, if any?

_____

_____

_____

_____

After learning about these costs and doing strategies that provided only temporary relief, how can you begin to show up in a manner that aligns with how you would like to live your life?

_____

_____

_____

_____

Check In		
I'm feeling a sense of fear and panic.	**STOP**
I'm feeling intense rage toward myself and others.	**STOP**
I'm feeling hopeless and worse than I did before.	**STOP**
I'm feeling uncomfortable and anxious.	**GROUNDING**
I'm feeling some uneasiness, but overall okay.	**CONTINUE**

What Is Traumatic Invalidation?

We receive *validation* when our feelings and experiences are accepted and supported by those around us. Alternatively, it can be painful to express your feelings only to be ignored. *Invalidation* may have occurred when the people around you failed to recognize the cues that something was amiss or misconstrued your disclosure of the abuse as lying. Invalidation may have impacted your self-worth, causing you to believe that your feelings are unimportant, which in turn may have contributed to an attempt to avoid painful emotions, thoughts, and memories.

Invalidation over a long period of time can be traumatizing, especially when you realize it negatively affects your understanding of yourself and your ability to participate in the world. If you were frequently told your feelings or experiences were unjustified, it makes sense that you might have difficulty accepting your own emotional experiences. You may feel insecure and have difficulty trusting your own feelings. Ultimately, you may have learned to ignore or restrain your feelings, thoughts, or memories as a way of coping with being invalidated.

Emotions are responsible for communicating with you and motivating your behavior. When you're in touch with your emotions, you gain a greater understanding of yourself and your surroundings. For instance, if you're in an unsafe situation, fear is a signal that you may be at risk; sadness is a signal that you may need to pay attention to yourself or seek support from others.

Although avoiding difficult emotions temporarily suppresses them, they become increasingly difficult to ignore over time. This can cause some survivors to turn to unhealthy methods of avoiding emotions, such as substance abuse. In addition, you must exert substantial effort to avoid your emotions, and as the emotions you're avoiding become stronger, you must exert increased effort to suppress them. The result is that you may not have much energy left to devote to the meaningful things in your life, such as your family, friends, career, and activities that you enjoy. Further, concentrating your energy on avoiding emotions may actually interfere with your ability to manage other emotions, such as disappointment and annoyance. There is also research suggesting that avoidant coping contributes to chronic worry and anxiety (Tull et al. 2011).

Developing Your Sense of Self

How you view yourself and the beliefs you hold about yourself can influence your ability to accept yourself as you are. Your sense of self is derived from how you value and perceive yourself, which is determined by your attitudes and beliefs about yourself. You may compare yourself to others, refrain from sharing your feelings out of fear of rejection, or feel undeserving of love. If this is the case for you, you are not alone.

Following sexual trauma, you may continue to experience feelings of self-doubt, which can lead to feelings of worthlessness, shame, guilt, and low self-esteem. These feelings can show up as an internal voice in your head that says, "You're not lovable, you're not capable, and you should have done A or B to stop the abuse." These thoughts and feelings can negatively affect your confidence at school and work, and especially in your relationships with others.

A healthy sense of self, on the other hand, can help you: accept yourself as you are, make decisions, assert yourself, recognize your strengths, show compassion toward yourself, and believe that you deserve happiness. Because your beliefs about yourself can have a profound impact on your feelings, thoughts, and behavior, it's important to be honest with yourself.

Schemas

In order to understand how sexual abuse may have influenced your beliefs, let's dig deeper. *Schemas* are narratives and beliefs that we create about ourselves and our relationships with others (Young, Kiodko, and Welshaar 2003). Schemas are essentially representations of the core beliefs you hold about yourself and the world that you do not question. The development of schemas starts in childhood, and for those who have experienced childhood sexual abuse, these narratives may have been crafted to help us understand what was occurring.

Messages from those who have hurt you may also contribute to the development of your schemas. For example, if you were told, "You deserve to be hurt because you did something wrong," you might carry this message with you into adulthood.

Once a schema develops, it's likely to remain the predominant way in which you perceive yourself and other people. Schemas are difficult to change and can create distortions in your thinking when you assume they are true in every situation. Though as much as schemas endure once they are formed, you may not always be aware of them. Incredibly, even schemas you're not aware of can surface when you're triggered by a particular event. In this case, your schema may contribute to your inability to cope with uncomfortable thoughts, feelings, and core beliefs.

A schema may have reactivated an ingrained belief about yourself if you've experienced moments of fear, shame, or despair that led to negative thoughts about yourself. Understanding the underlying causes of these beliefs is vital, since the intensity and pain of these feelings may contribute to anxiety, depression, PTSD symptoms, and impaired interpersonal relationships (Leahy 2019).

Let's look at some common schemas and associated beliefs so that you can consider whether your ability to accept yourself may be influenced by a specific trauma-related schema. Although the examples provided here are of typical thoughts that survivors might have, they do not in any way represent all possible related thoughts within a given schema. Take a moment to review the chart and see if any of the examples presented resonate with you. In the far right column, place a checkmark in the box if the statement reflects a belief or thought that you currently hold.

Common Schemas

Schema	Core Belief	Example	✓
Abandonment/ Instability	Believing that significant people in your life are unstable or unreliable	"People will leave me." "The world is unsafe."	
Mistrust/Abuse	Expecting that you'll be harmed through abuse or neglect	"I cannot trust myself." "If I let people in, they will hurt me."	
Emotional deprivation	Expecting that the need for emotional support will not be met	"People will not understand or protect me."	

Schema	Core Belief	Example	✓
Defectiveness/ Shame	Believing that you are defective or unlovable	"I am unlovable." "There is something wrong with me."	
Social isolation/ Alienation	Believing that you do not belong to a group or are different from others	"I'm not like other people." "I don't connect or fit in."	
Dependence	Believing that you are incompetent or helpless	"I need them around me because I'm not capable of doing things on my own."	
Failure	Believing that you are inadequate	"I am a failure." "I will not succeed even if I try."	
Entitlement/ Grandiosity	Believing that you deserve privileges and are superior to others	"I deserve special treatment." "I am better than them."	
Self-sacrifice/ Subjugation	Trying to satisfy the needs of others at the expense of your own desires, or surrendering control to others due to real or perceived coercion	"I'll ignore what I want because I want to make them happy." "If I don't give in, they will hurt me."	
Unrelenting standards	Believing that you must meet a very high standard to avoid the criticism of others	"I have to be perfect, or they will judge and criticize me."	

Recognizing Your Schemas

All of us hold some kind of belief about ourselves, whether we are aware of it or not. The questions in the next exercise will assist you in examining the feelings and thoughts you may have associated with your core beliefs, so that you can decide if you hold that particular schema or belief. Read each question, then place a checkmark in the Yes or No columns that best describes your answer. You may find it helpful to use the reflection prompts after the charts to recall situations when these thoughts were prominent in your mind. The reflection questions can increase your awareness of circumstances in which these beliefs may be activated. As there is no right or wrong answer, just be honest with yourself while completing the exercise.

Please note that this exercise is not intended to be a comprehensive schema assessment. For a complete schema questionnaire, see the book *Prisoners of Belief: Exposing and Changing Beliefs That Control Your Life* (McKay and Fanning 1991).

Abandonment/Instability

Questions	Yes	No
1. Would you describe the people in your life as unstable and unreliable?		
2. When you were growing up, did you believe that your family wasn't there to protect you?		
3. Do you often feel uncertain about whether you can rely on those around you?		
4. Are you fearful that your loved ones will leave you or reject you?		
5. Do you find it difficult to maintain lasting relationships?		

If you're worried that you may be abandoned by those you care about, describe how this fear impacts your current relationships.

_____

_____

_____

_____

Mistrust/Abuse

Questions	Yes	No
1. Is it your experience that people often hurt you, take advantage of you, or consistently let you down?		

Questions	Yes	No
2. When it comes to trusting, do you find it difficult?		
3. Would you consider yourself to be on guard in order to prevent yourself from being lied to or retaliated against by others?		
4. Do you believe that most people will not keep their promises, therefore you cannot rely on them to follow through?		
5. Are you concerned that other people will not treat you with respect or will hurt you?		

Take a moment to recall the first time you felt that you could not trust those around you. What made you feel unable to trust in this situation? How has not being able to trust those around you affected your current relationships?

_____

_____

_____

_____

Emotional Deprivation

Questions	Yes	No
1. Are you concerned that you'll not be loved or cared for, and that your emotional needs will not be met?		
2. Would you consider your family members to be cold and distant rather than nurturing?		
3. Are you convinced that no one will be able to provide you with the care and attention you need?		
4. Are you dissatisfied with the quality of your intimate relationships?		

Questions	Yes	No
5. Are you concerned that you can't rely on your friends for advice or emotional support?		

In what ways have you felt unsupported or uncared for during your life?

_____

_____

_____

_____

Defectiveness/Shame

Questions	Yes	No
1. Are you often critical of your appearance or view yourself as defective?		
2. Is there a part of you that feels unworthy of love, attention, or respect from others?		
3. Do you believe you don't matter in this world?		
4. Would you consider your needs unworthy of being met?		
5. If people knew more about you, do you think they would like you?		

What would you say to your younger self who felt unlovable and defective?

_____

_____

_____

_____

Social Isolation/Alienation

Questions	Yes	No
1. Do you frequently feel out of place in your family, community, or group environment?		
2. Do you feel that you're different from your friends and don't fit in with them?		
3. Are you concerned that people don't accept you as you are?		
4. In a large group, do you often have difficulty approaching or speaking to others?		
5. Is it your belief that people don't include you in their activities?		

Write down all the characteristics that you value about yourself that may be different from others.

_____

_____

_____

_____

Dependence

Questions	Yes	No
1. When you're faced with many situations, do you feel incompetent and unable to accomplish the task at hand?		
2. Do you consider certain people to be essential to your survival?		
3. Are you consistently in need of or asking for help from others?		
4. When you're not sure what to do, do you often feel helpless?		

Questions	Yes	No
5. Would you say that you lack the confidence to handle most problems on your own?		

Do you have any advice you would give to your younger self regarding your ability to handle problems on your own?

_____

_____

_____

_____

Failure

Questions	Yes	No
1. Do you believe that whatever you attempt, you will fail?		
2. When you trust your own judgment, do you believe that you often make the wrong decision?		
3. Do you avoid taking on challenges for fear that you won't be able to succeed?		
4. Is it difficult for you to perform well under stress?		
5. Do you think it's difficult for you to accomplish many tasks and that you sometimes fail to perform many tasks well?		

Make a list of situations in which you fear failure (for example, at work, in relationships, in school). Next to each item on the list, describe something you did well in that situation and that you're proud of. For example, "I fear doing something wrong at work—I received a promotion recently."

_____

_____

_____

_____

Self-Sacrifice/Subjugation

Questions	Yes	No
1. Do you always strive to please others and put their needs before your own?		
2. Do you believe that others are better able to provide you with care than you are?		
3. Do you believe that everything you do requires the approval of others?		
4. Is it common for you to avoid disagreeing with others and to keep your opinions to yourself?		
5. Is it difficult for you to express your own wants and needs?		

It's possible that you may not know your current needs if you've become accustomed to putting others' needs above your own. Take time now to express opinions that you've not shared or to list your own needs and desires.

_____

_____

_____

_____

Reflect

Take a moment to reflect on all of your answers. See if you can increase your awareness of the schemas you hold and the ways you may have attempted to make emotions go away.

Which three schemas scored the most yes answers, with at least three yes responses out of five?

_____

_____

_____

In what triggering situations do you feel the schemas might show up or have shown up before?

_____

_____

_____

_____

When you reflect on all the times you've experienced the schema feeling, have you ever done anything that helped you cope with the feeling?

_____

_____

_____

_____

It is possible that your efforts to cope with schema feelings and thoughts have not been successful as a long-term "fix." Although these strategies often work temporarily, they often hurt you more in the long run. When schema feelings are triggered, can you think of something else you might do to deal with the situation that is more aligned with how you want to show up in the world?

_____

_____

_____

_____

_____

I'm feeling a sense of fear and panic.	**STOP**
I'm feeling intense rage toward myself and others.	**STOP**
I'm feeling hopeless and worse than I did before.	**STOP**
I'm feeling uncomfortable and anxious.	**GROUNDING**
I'm feeling some uneasiness, but overall okay.	**CONTINUE**

How Do You Deal with Schemas?

Think about the schemas you identified in the previous exercise. Over the years, you've probably come up with ways to cope with these painful beliefs and feelings, even if you don't realize it. Some common coping strategies seem as if they're helping, but they're actually making things worse. For example, withdrawing socially or using substances are coping strategies that may work in the short term, but they can leave you isolated and maintain the schema rather than provide long-term relief from the pain.

One of the most commonly reported coping strategies among survivors is *schema avoidance*. There are many forms of avoidance coping strategies. With schema avoidance coping, rather than addressing unwanted feelings or triggers, we try to push them away. This differs from moments when we need to disconnect from others and engage in a private activity such as reading, taking a bath, or playing a game. The key difference is that these helpful self-soothing techniques invite us to decompress rather than avoid.

To better understand the differences between avoidance types, it can be helpful to explore which, if any, of the following avoidance coping strategies you currently use. Use the next chart to identify when you may have used a schema avoidance coping strategy and whether it provided temporary or long-term relief.

Common Schema Avoidance Coping Strategies

Avoidance coping	Description	When have you used this strategy?	Temporary or long-term relief? If so, how?
Social or psychological withdrawal	May withdraw by isolating or disconnecting from others; may escape through dissociation, numbness, or denial		
Excessive autonomy	May demonstrate an exaggerated focus on independence and self-reliance, rather than on involvement with others		
Compulsive stimulation seeking	May seek excitement or distraction through compulsive shopping, sex, gambling, risk-taking, physical activity, and so forth		
Addictive self-soothing	May use addictive substances or behaviors, such as alcohol, drugs, overeating, excessive masturbation, and so forth to escape		

A schema may trigger you to use other forms of coping, such as how you approach rather than avoid the situation. It's not uncommon for survivors to act out, overcompensate, or surrender in response to painful emotions triggered by a schema.

You may have had moments when you felt the need to defend yourself, but your anger resulted in you blaming the other person rather than explaining how you felt. At other times, you may have felt such a powerful need for approval that you chose to disregard your own feelings in favor of the needs of others. These coping strategies are similar to avoidance coping in that rather than addressing these emotions, you attempt to "fix" them in any way you can. Perhaps this is not the case for you. You may find it helpful, however, to determine whether you're currently utilizing any of the following *attack or surrender coping strategies*.

Use the next chart to identify when you may have used an attack or surrender coping strategy and whether it provided temporary or long-term relief.

Attack or Surrender Coping Strategies

Attack or surrender coping	Description	When have you used this strategy?	Short- or long-term relief? If so, how?
Aggression/ Hostility	May counterattack through blaming, attacking, or criticizing others		
Dominance/ Excessive self-assertion	May attempt to control others to accomplish goals		
Recognition- seeking/ Status-seeking	May overcompensate through seeking high achievement or attention		

Attack or surrender coping	Description	When have you used this strategy?	Short- or long-term relief? If so, how?
Manipulation/ Exploitation	May use manipulation, seduction, or dishonesty to meet own needs		
Passive-aggressiveness/ Rebellion	May appear compliant, yet punishes others by pouting, complaining, or rebellion through procrastination		
Compliance/ Dependence	May avoid conflict or rely on others through people-pleasing		

Reflect

These schema coping behaviors may not apply to you, or you may not be sure if and when they apply to you. You may feel overwhelmed at this point, which is understandable. Feel free to take a break from this workbook whenever you need to. At the present moment, only you know what is best for you. You are the expert of your own situation. It's likely that this exercise has increased your awareness of any schema coping strategies you may be using. It may now be helpful to consider how these behaviors might appear in your day-to-day life and identify more helpful coping strategies.

Have you ever handled these situations differently when the schema was triggered in the past? If so, how did you handle it?

_____

_____

_____

_____

When you experience a schema feeling, what could you do to not be overwhelmed by it? Would reminding yourself that the pain will end help you get through?

_____

_____

_____

_____

Helpful Schema Coping Behaviors

The following are examples of helpful ways to cope with difficult situations. You may wish to add your own alternative coping strategies on the lines provided based on what you think might be supportive in managing the overwhelming feelings and thoughts associated with schemas. You can turn to this list when you need a reminder of a beneficial coping strategy tailored to your unique needs.

Examples of helpful coping behaviors:

- Setting boundaries

- Reassuring yourself with supportive thoughts (for example, "I'm doing the best I can.")

- Calling a support person

- Soothing yourself through your senses

  - *Sight/Smell:* Lighting candles or smelling scents

  - *Taste:* Eating mindfully

- *Touch:* Rubbing a soft material
- *Sounds:* Listening to music or sounds around you

- Journaling

- _____

- _____

- _____

- _____

- _____

When a schema feeling arises, I believe the following alternative coping behaviors will be helpful:

1. _____

2. _____

3. _____

4. _____

5. _____

6. _____

7. _____

I'm feeling a sense of fear and panic.	**STOP**
I'm feeling intense rage toward myself and others.	**STOP**
I'm feeling hopeless and worse than I did before.	**STOP**
I'm feeling uncomfortable and anxious.	**GROUNDING**
I'm feeling some uneasiness, but overall okay.	**CONTINUE**

Understanding Your Schema Coping Style

To complete this exercise, select the schema that you had the most yes responses to on the Recognizing Your Schemas exercise. Then, answer the questions based on that schema.

Which schema is showing up most in your life?

_____

What emotions do you experience when this schema appears?

_____

_____

_____

If you could float back in time to the first time you felt the schema of _____

and the emotions of _____, when would it have been?

_____

_____

_____

How would you describe a recent situation that may have triggered this schema and emotion?

_____

_____

_____

_____

What are the barriers that prevent you from accepting these difficult emotions or living the life you value and desire?

_____

_____

_____

_____

Based on the schema coping behaviors you listed previously, which behaviors have proven most helpful for you? What coping behaviors limit you?

_____

_____

_____

_____

Did you experience any negative consequences when you employed these schema coping behaviors? If so, what were the outcomes?

_____

_____

_____

_____

Earlier, you listed alternative schema coping behaviors that you consider helpful. Which of those strategies do you think would be most effective for this specific schema? How likely are you to practice it on a daily basis?

_____

_____

_____

_____

Schemas and Self-Awareness

It is likely that this chapter touched on a part of you that may feel uncomfortable, painful, or even cause you to want to stop reading this book. This feeling is entirely understandable, as you've explored parts of yourself that you may not have been unaware of, were unwilling to acknowledge, or simply did not wish to accept. You now understand that what occurred has left an impact—yes—but you're not who you were back then. Even though you may still respond to triggers as you did in childhood, you are now a survivor. If you're willing to explore how your trauma schemas affect your ability to lead a full and meaningful life, the wisdom gained can be helpful in healing.

There are times when events occur and we react without any conscious thought or understanding of why we responded the way we did. For those who have experienced sexual abuse, this behavior may be due to our autonomic nervous system's response to stress: _fight, flight, freeze,_ or _fawn._ It's imperative to remember that our schema coping behaviors are a natural reaction to trauma; your brain was forced to calculate how it should react in any given circumstance. The more you are willing to sit with your feelings and thoughts and resist the urge to push them down, the more you can move toward healing.

It's important to understand how these schemas might show up in your daily life and what aspects of your life may be maintaining them. The journaling exercise that follows will assist you in assessing the extent to which you're using these schemas every day.

Journaling

Awareness can bring up thoughts, memories, and feelings you may not have been conscious of or have forgotten about. It can be helpful to write about your experience and feelings, especially if you've had difficulty telling others about the abuse. Focusing on sensory details that occurred during the abuse can help you identify the things that may be triggering to you now. For some survivors, reliving the experience can be too difficult and invoke fear. In this case, use this journaling activity to write about how you think certain memories are currently affecting your life. The choice is yours.

Please write for as long as you can—at least fifteen minutes. It can be helpful to set a timer. It's okay if you run out of things to say before the timer goes off. If this happens, don't stop. Instead, you can draw or write about what you're thinking or feeling (for example, "I don't like writing" or "I need to do laundry"). Stop writing after the fifteen minutes is up and reflect on what you wrote. If you think you'll need more space than what's provided here, grab paper now, before you begin, so you can continue on those pages.

_____

_____

_____

_____

_____

_____

_____

_____

_____

_____

_____

I'm feeling a sense of fear and panic.	**STOP**
I'm feeling intense rage toward myself and others.	**STOP**
I'm feeling hopeless and worse than I did before.	**STOP**
I'm feeling uncomfortable and anxious.	**GROUNDING**
I'm feeling some uneasiness, but overall okay.	**CONTINUE**

Check In

Tying It All Together

Part of your healing process involves acknowledging how past events have shaped how you think, feel, and respond to stressors. Remembering the experiences and feelings that you encountered during childhood sexual abuse can be painful, and it's not uncommon for adults to want to avoid this part of healing. Not all survivors will want to recall those events, and some memories will remain unclear even if you want to recall them. Regardless of the circumstances, you can rebuild hope, gain a sense of control, and heal from the long-term effects of abuse.

By becoming aware and accepting where you are and who you are, you can manage emotions. Despite the adversity you've faced, you will rebuild hope for a better future and heal. The next chapter will explore how your perception of yourself and the world around you may influence your capacity to accept and embrace yourself.

Reflect on your current feelings and goals for understanding yourself by answering the following questions:

What feelings arose as I worked through this section?

_____

_____

_____

_____

What aspects were outside of my awareness before that I am aware of now? What aspects still confuse me?

_____

_____

_____

_____

What exercises were too difficult for me to do that I would like to return to later?

_____

_____

_____

_____

What triggers have I identified? What sensations, feelings, thoughts, or urges have surfaced that I found difficult to allow to be part of my experience? What might be holding me back?

_____

_____

_____

_____

What do I need to do to take care of myself and ensure that I'm practicing self-care (for example, spend time outdoors, meditate, take a break from this workbook)?

_____

_____

_____

_____

_____

On a scale of 1 to 10, rate your level of hope both *before* you began this chapter and *currently*.
 	
    1 = feeling completely hopeless
 	
    10 = feeling extremely hopeful
	Before the chapter _____
	
	After the chapter _____

CHAPTER 2

Practicing Self-Acceptance

"When we criticize ourselves, we are both the attacked and the attacker."

—Kristin Neff

A state of *self-acceptance* is exactly what its name implies: a state of becoming completely at ease with yourself. A true sense of self-acceptance consists of accepting yourself for who you are without qualification, conditions, or exceptions (Seltzer 2008). Self-acceptance occurs when you're aware of your own strengths and weaknesses, and have an understanding of and satisfaction with who you are.

Right now, this all might sound very difficult, and you aren't expected to just be able to find this kind of self-acceptance right away. You need support along your journey, and I will guide you there throughout this workbook.

Self-acceptance is a critical component of healing. If you lack self-acceptance, you may often question your own thoughts and feelings, and assume even valid feelings are not valid. In addition, sometimes negative thoughts and feelings are internalized, which can lead to self-blame (Karakurt and Silver 2014; Kaye-Tzadok and Davidson-Arad 2016). These are states of self we don't want to be in.

To be clear, self-acceptance is not the same as self-esteem. *Self-esteem* is the way you value and perceive yourself, whereas self-acceptance goes beyond embracing only the good and positive aspects of yourself; it requires acceptance of the negative and the unpleasant aspects as well. In other words, with self-acceptance you're able to acknowledge your weaknesses and limitations without judgment, and this does not in any way affect your ability to embrace yourself as you are.

Accepting all negative aspects of yourself can be difficult, and you're not wrong in thinking that! But with practice it becomes easier. One way to help you accept the traits and habits you find undesirable is to build *self-compassion*. After abuse, it can be difficult to practice self-compassion. But if you practice self-compassion and develop self-acceptance, you will be more able to take responsibility for your feelings, thoughts, and actions—and practice self-love. By reducing or stopping judging yourself, you'll be able to establish a stronger sense of self-confidence and a more positive sense of who you are.

How Trauma Impacts Self-Acceptance

Trauma can impact the way you perceive and accept yourself. As an example, if you were told that you deserved abuse because you did something wrong, weren't kind enough, or were selfish, you may struggle to fully accept yourself. If you were surrounded by unaccepting and uncompassionate adults, you may hold onto how they saw you as a child. As you have grown older, it's understandable that you may have become more critical of yourself and internalized the rejection you experienced from those who abused you or did not protect you from harm. When you've grown up in such an environment, it's easy to blame and berate yourself for your mistakes.

Additionally, survivors often experience feelings of guilt and shame as a result of their experiences. In the aftermath of being sexually abused, it's natural to feel these emotions, especially if you've found yourself questioning your response. Perhaps you felt powerless and could not say no or resist physically, yet you feel guilty for this response. In some cases, you might feel shame for becoming sexually aroused even though you disliked what was happening to you. These emotions make sense, but they can also act as a barrier to you becoming more accepting of yourself. If, when you consider the trauma, you experience guilty feelings or shame, and these emotions are followed by negative thoughts about yourself, this self-critical view of yourself stands as a barrier to self-acceptance.

Keep in mind that your past has helped you get to where you are today. Thus, you were provided with both strengths and susceptibilities as a result of the experience. When you embrace your past, it can help you identify the things most meaningful to you in the present.

Assessing Your Level of Self-Acceptance

The following exercise is intended to help you assess your current level of self-acceptance. It will help you identify the areas of your life that have been most affected by abuse and the progress you've already made toward self-acceptance. It includes statements that describe common feelings and experiences of survivors of childhood sexual abuse.

This is an ideal exercise to do periodically, as what you mark today may be different a month or a year from now. The healing process changes over time. When you observe an area that you would have marked more negatively in the past but feel more confident about today, take a moment to appreciate the progress that you've already made. It is important to celebrate your accomplishments throughout your journey of healing.

To assess where you are now regarding self-acceptance, read each statement in the chart (adapted from Davis 1990, 124–128). Then, check the column that most aligns with how you currently feel:

	Constantly	Often	Sometimes	Seldom	Not at all
I don't think my feelings are valid.					
I deserve to be unhappy.					
I feel unlovable.					
I'm often confused and don't trust my own feelings.					
I deserve to be happy.					
I often think there is something wrong with me or that I'm damaged.					
I try to be perfect in everything I do, so that no one will know how much of a failure I feel I am.					
I'm afraid my romantic partner will leave me if they know how hopeless I feel.					
I view my body as ugly and try to cover it up as much as possible.					
I admire who I am and believe I am worthy of love.					
I trust my gut feelings and often find my instincts are accurate.					
I believe mistakes are part of growth and don't feel as though I need to be perfect.					
My feelings are valid.					
I'm comfortable in my skin, and I don't feel the need to hide my body.					

You may feel some uneasiness or discomfort when reading these statements. The purpose of this exercise, however, is to determine whether you accept yourself as you are, as well as to identify any areas you may need to explore in order to deepen your self-acceptance. There is a reason you feel this way, and looking at your feelings closely is an important step toward healing.

Consider the answers you listed in the previous chart when answering the questions that follow. If it is too overwhelming to do that at this moment in time, stop and come back to it when you feel you're ready.

The areas in which I have the greatest self-acceptance is

_____

_____

_____

_____

_____

I may be struggling with self-acceptance in the areas of

_____

_____

_____

_____

_____

I'm feeling a sense of fear and panic.	STOP
I'm feeling intense rage toward myself and others.	STOP
I'm feeling hopeless and worse than I did before.	STOP
I'm feeling uncomfortable and anxious.	GROUNDING
I'm feeling some uneasiness, but overall okay.	CONTINUE

CHECK IN

Self-Acceptance and Developing Hope

Maintaining hope in the aftermath of abuse can be challenging. It's not uncommon to feel hopeful about certain aspects of your life while feeling hopeless about others. The experience of sexual abuse can often lead to self-blame and feeling a lack of control, both of which diminish hope that the future will be better. When you realize that you have willingness to make your life better and you begin to believe in yourself, hope will develop.

One way to rebuild hope back into your life is to identify the areas that you feel capable of changing or accepting, forgiving yourself, and establishing new goals for coping and adapting. As simple as it sounds, it is not. It may be easy for you to feel compassion for someone else, but when it comes to showing compassion to yourself, you may believe that you don't deserve the same kindness and compassion as those around you. In these thoughts and feelings, you may hear your trauma voice (inner critic) telling you that you deserve the guilt and shame you feel, which may be the result of your schemas and the feeling that "I should have prevented it." The trauma voice, which you'll learn more about in chapter 3, can interfere with your ability to accept yourself and be compassionate toward yourself.

As you learn how to take care of yourself in a loving and compassionate manner, you'll remind yourself that you are worthy of your focus, attention, and love. Mindfulness techniques and coping strategies discussed in this workbook can be incorporated into your daily routine to build a foundation of self-acceptance and self-compassion. In the proceeding sections, you'll practice different coping strategies through activities that will help minimize stress and increase your sense of self-compassion, acceptance, and hope.

Reassessing Your Level of Self-Acceptance

This exercise invites you to assess where you are now, how hopeful you feel, and your areas of strengths, so that you can build upon your strengths and establish goals accordingly. To complete this exercise, review your answers from the previous exercise.

What areas are you most hopeful about being able to accept or change?

_____

_____

_____

_____

_____

List the areas that seem to create a feeling of hopelessness, leading you to have uncertainty about whether they can be accepted or changed.

_____

_____

_____

Despite what has happened to you, you survived. Survival takes strength and determination. There may be certain attributes that you possess that have allowed you to get to where you are today. By identifying your strengths, you can take a moment to feel deserving and good about yourself. It's a way to acknowledge the characteristics and skills that have enabled you to heal. In the following chart, circle all the characteristics that you possess.

Persistent	Empathetic	Able to set boundaries	Self-sufficient
Courageous	Patient	Realistic	Hard-working
Creative	Generous	Independent	Loyal
Optimistic	Self-confident	Resourceful	Considerate
Intuitive	Self-disciplined	Fair	Kind
Humble	Open-minded	Honest	Resilient
Thankful	Leader	Trustworthy	Hopeful
Humorous	Lifelong learner	Survivor	Determined

Look at the qualities that you circled. Are you surprised by some of the ones you chose? If this was a difficult task for you, that's okay. It can be awkward to think of yourself in a positive light, especially if you're overwhelmed by the negative effects of abuse. It's important to accept that even if you have a difficult time recognizing your own strengths, your survival depended on your inner strength. Therefore, whether you can see them now or not is not as important as acknowledging that your inner strength is what has brought you to this point in your life. If you were unable to identify any strengths, ask members of your support system what they see in you, and then try this exercise again.

Check In		
I'm feeling a sense of fear and panic.		**STOP**
I'm feeling intense rage toward myself and others.		**STOP**
I'm feeling hopeless and worse than I did before.		**STOP**
I'm feeling uncomfortable and anxious.		**GROUNDING**
I'm feeling some uneasiness, but overall okay.		**CONTINUE**

Mindful Acceptance

A key component to self-acceptance is the ability to recognize your emotions and how your response to these emotions can affect your ability to tolerate distressing situations. You can gain a deeper understanding of your emotions by learning to observe and respond to emotional activation without reacting, judging, or controlling it (McKay and West 2016). A good way to accomplish this is to become aware of and accept all aspects of your emotions while recognizing that you are not your emotions. This is the practice of *mindful acceptance*, which teaches you how to act as an observer of your emotions. In turn, and over time, this increases your tolerance for distressing emotions.

A common misconception is that emotions are just feelings (such as sadness, anger, fear), when in fact they can manifest as sensations, thoughts, and urges as well. Being present with distressing emotions can be challenging, as it is human nature to avoid pain. The process of becoming aware of your emotions, however, also increases awareness of your urges to react, avoid, or attempt to control them.

It is important to emphasize that acceptance does not mean that you need to approve of your emotions or their triggers. Nevertheless, a mindful acceptance practice allows you to give yourself permission to experience emotions by teaching you how to respond to them in a way that is more beneficial to your life and well-being.

Mindful Acceptance Meditation

You can try mindful acceptance by completing the following exercise. You will practice accepting sensations in your body, identifying feelings, watching your thoughts, and noticing urges to react to these emotions. It's best if you can set aside at least ten minutes each day to practice without disruptions. You can do this meditation when you're resting or when you're experiencing emotional distress. If reading and practicing at the same time is cumbersome, you may record yourself saying these steps and play them back to yourself, or you can access a free audio track of this practice at http://www.newharbinger.com/53790.

1.   Consider sitting in a comfortable position and closing your eyes or gazing at something in front of you.

2.   Observe any sensations in your body for a few moments. Observe your body until you identify a sensation (for example, tension, heat, racing heart, numbness) and pay attention to it. See if you can allow the sensation to be as it is. Notice whether this sensation is changing, staying the same, or if there is a certain tension present. Allow yourself to relax into the sensation.

3.   If you can, try to identify and label a feeling that you can associate with the sensation (for example, fear, sadness, anxiousness). Try not to judge or react to the feeling.

4.   For at least three minutes, observe each thought as it arises. There is a constant stream of thoughts coming from our brain, and the key is to not get wrapped up in thoughts. Instead, notice the thought and simply say, "There's a thought," and then let that thought go. Return to present moment and wait for the next thought to emerge. If you're having difficulty letting the thought go, acknowledge it as a "sticky thought" and then release it. Spend the next few minutes observing your thoughts.

5.   Now, for the next thirty seconds, notice if there is an urge associated with your sensations, feelings, or thoughts. An urge may arise to do something or refrain from doing something. Let the urge just sit with you for a moment. Observe how it feels to not act on the urge.

6.   If you have not reached ten minutes, repeat steps 2 through 5 again.

7.   Take several deep breaths and slowly open your eyes.

After you've been practicing the mindful acceptance meditation *for a week or two,* you'll be better able to identify and recognize specific triggers to your distress, observe your sensations and feelings, and recognize reoccurring thoughts and urges that may be difficult to release or acknowledge.

The following charts will help you record your observations and your experiences related to specific distress triggers. Fill them out *after* you've been practicing the mindful acceptance meditation daily for *at least a week.* If you have difficulty with this exercise, return to your mindful acceptance meditation and record what you observe after a session of practice. A sample is provided to show how you'll record your sensations, feelings, thoughts, and urges that you noticed while practicing mindful acceptance when a triggering event happens.

Sample – Distressing Event

Triggers	My partner said that I do everything the hard way.
Sensations	Chest tightness
Feelings	Anger and sadness
Thoughts	"I'm not good enough."
Urges	Isolate and push the thoughts and feelings away

Now it's your turn. Record the sensations, feelings, thoughts, and urges that you notice while practicing mindful acceptance during two triggering events.

Distressing Event #1

Triggers	
Sensations	
Feelings	
Thoughts	
Urges	

Distressing Event #2

Triggers	
Sensations	
Feelings	
Thoughts	
Urges	

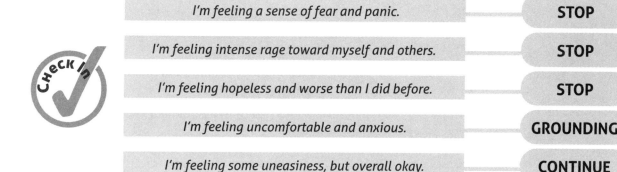

I'm feeling a sense of fear and panic.	**STOP**
I'm feeling intense rage toward myself and others.	**STOP**
I'm feeling hopeless and worse than I did before.	**STOP**
I'm feeling uncomfortable and anxious.	**GROUNDING**
I'm feeling some uneasiness, but overall okay.	**CONTINUE**

Tying It All Together

In the process of healing, it may be difficult for you to identify your weaknesses without judging yourself. In spite of this, you can begin to accept yourself as you are simply by acknowledging the positive and less-favorable aspects of yourself.

It is not surprising that you have certain reactions to stress that evoke intense emotions and the urge to avoid these feelings and thoughts. In recognizing these tendencies and acknowledging that they may act as barriers to you increasing self-acceptance, you're setting yourself up for greater meaning and fulfillment in your life. Remember that your past, as terrifying as it was, has helped you reach this point in your life. You may be reading this workbook because you've now decided to embrace your past. That takes strength, courage, and a desire for growth. All of which will help you decide the things that are important to you, so that you can recognize the things most meaningful to you in the present.

This is a difficult journey, and it can be overwhelming at times, but you can heal. This starts by understanding how trauma may have impacted your response to stressors. In the next chapter, you'll learn about the trauma voice and how it may have helped you survive and cope. Additionally, you'll identify any unmet needs and explore other helpful ways of coping.

The questions below are meant to give you an opportunity to reflect on your present feelings and goals pertaining to self-acceptance.

What feelings arose as I worked through this section?

_____

_____

_____

_____

_____

What aspects were outside of my awareness before that I'm aware of now? What aspects still confuse me?

_____

_____

_____

_____

_____

_____

What exercises were too difficult for me to do that I would like to return to later?

_____

_____

_____

_____

_____

Based on the strengths I identified, what aspects of myself am I willing to accept? These are traits and habits that I'm hopeful that I can continue (or change, if need be).

_____

_____

_____

_____

_____

What aspects am I unable to accept because I'm uncertain if I can change or improve them? What might be holding me back?

_____

_____

_____

_____

_____

What do I need to do to take care of myself and ensure that I'm practicing self-care (for example, spend time outdoors, meditate, take a break from this workbook)?

_____

_____

_____

_____

_____

On a scale of 1 to 10, rate your level of hope both *before* you began this chapter and *currently*.	
1 = feeling completely hopeless	Before the chapter _____
10 = feeling extremely hopeful	After the chapter _____

CHAPTER 3

Your Voice of Survival

"With every negative judgment, every attack, your inner critic weakens you and tears down any good feelings you may have about yourself."

—Beverly Engel

In this chapter, you'll learn how to recognize your *trauma voice*, which is the voice that may have steered you toward certain ways of coping so you could survive and that may be influencing your behavior today. As you become aware of the effects of abuse on brain development, you're better able to explore any unmet needs that may guide your behaviors, thoughts, and feelings.

Although not all feelings of danger are unfounded, it's important to recognize that some reactions to danger may be false alarms. As an analogy, imagine you're making popcorn when suddenly a smoke detector goes off. The sound of the alarm wouldn't urge you to run from the building. Instead, you would check the burning popcorn and then open a window. You would remain calm knowing it was just a false alarm.

Our minds produce false alarms too. When this happens, though, our bodies react with a trauma response—an autonomic physiological reaction to an event that is perceived as stressful, frightening, or threatening—even when there is no present danger. To prevent a trauma response during false alarms, you can notice your trauma voice and begin to recognize when it is telling you to cope in an unhelpful way. This will help you heal and make better choices.

Trauma can affect brain development and functioning. Your experience of childhood sexual abuse may affect how your brain functions when you perceive a lack of safety as an adult. Changes in your brain and limbic system (the part of the brain involved in our behavioral and emotional responses) can result in:

- Feeling as though you are in constant survival mode

- Perceiving the world as unsafe

- Staying alert to noises, your surroundings, or perceived threats

- A belief that your subconscious thoughts are your rational thoughts, when in reality, these thoughts may not be rational at all but simply reactions to an unsafe environment

Do any of these states of being resonate with you? If they do, when do you notice slipping into these behaviors or having these feelings?

_____

_____

_____

_____

A trauma response is involuntary. When something happens that your brain perceives as a threat, it activates the sympathetic nervous system and triggers an acute stress response that prepares your body to react. Among these responses are fight, flight, freeze, and fawn, which were discussed in chapter 1.

Essentially, your brain puts you in survival mode. It's trying to protect you from the threat. Even so, while you're in survival mode, it's quite common for you to experience self-defeating thoughts and feelings. This may lead you to use negative coping strategies, such as the misuse of substances or avoidant responses.

What Is a Trauma Voice?

Your trauma voice might sound or feel like the voice of the person who abused you, saying, "You're bad and deserve to be hurt," or it could be your own voice saying, "I don't belong, so I'll avoid others."

Your trauma voice can be activated by:

- A trigger, which can be a situation, feelings of shame or guilt, or feeling uncomfortable sensations in your body related to a trauma memory (somatic flashback)

- Your brain (limbic system) perceiving a threat and reacting to it as if you're in danger, even if it is a false alarm

You may be in trauma response mode even if the trauma occurred in childhood. And particularly if you're convinced that your thoughts are rational and true when perhaps they're not. These thoughts may in fact be the limbic system recognizing the thought and reacting to the stress or trigger. Increasing your awareness of the trauma voice will enable you to acknowledge this voice and identify it when it is speaking. By practicing awareness, you'll begin to understand that this voice is not part of your identity but a reaction to stress and abuse.

For instance, let's say you thought, "I feel like hiding my pain by drinking right now" or "I feel like I need to avoid interacting with people because they don't understand me." You can simply identify these statements for what they are: the trauma voice. Then label the thoughts, for example, "That is my trauma voice trying to help me cope by urging me to drink and avoid others."

Once you can recognize the trauma voice, you'll be able to replace a previous coping behavior (for example, drinking or avoidance) with an alternative behavior (for example, spending time outdoors or calling a support person on your list) and manage triggering thoughts (Younique Foundation 2017).

Take a moment to explore your trauma voice by responding to the following prompts:

In your own words, describe how you hear your trauma voice.

_____

_____

_____

_____

_____

Do you question whether this narrative about yourself is true? If so, how would you like to see yourself or what would you like to say to your trauma voice?

_____

_____

_____

_____

Your trauma voice helped keep you alive through the abuse. That voice had a purpose, and sometimes in order to let it go we have to thank it first. If you would like to express gratitude to your trauma voice for assisting in your survival, please use the lines below to express your gratitude.

_____

_____

_____

_____

Identifying Your Trauma Voice

In the following exercise, inspired by the work of Laura Davis (1990), you'll learn how to identify and accept your trauma voice. You'll also learn how to identify empowering and beneficial behaviors that will counteract what your trauma voice urged you to do. Before you get started, take a look at the examples of positive coping behaviors. Circle the ones that you enjoy or you would like to try, then see if you can come up with a few of your own.

Common Helpful Coping Strategies
(Alternative Behaviors)

Practice deep breathing	Meditation	Mindfulness activity
Exercise	Yoga	Write in a journal
Take a bath	Listen to music	Call a support person
Create a to-do list	Spend time outdoors	Spend time with a pet
Practice a hobby	Play a sport	Play a board game
Create art	Put a puzzle together	Read a book

Now, let's take a closer look at your trauma voice and trauma responses. Use the steps and examples to guide your practice.

1. Think of an event or situation from the past month where you felt particularly activated. In the first column of the chart, describe who you were with, what happened, and when it happened.

2. In the second column, identify the trauma voice. What was it saying to you?

3. Next, describe the behavior—the trauma response—that the trauma voice told you to do.

4. Look back at the list of Common Helpful Coping Strategies. Pick one to try and write it down in the fourth column.

5. Review the examples to help you complete the blank chart.

Trauma Voice and Response Chart – Sample

Event or situation Who? What? Where? When?	Trauma voice thought What was going through your mind?	Trauma response How did the trauma voice try to help you to cope?	Alternative behaviors What could you say and do to cope instead?
A stressful day at work ended with my boss criticizing my work.	"I feel like hiding my pain by drinking right now."	Urging me to drink alcohol	"My trauma voice is trying to help me deal with pain by telling me to drink alcohol. I'll get iced tea instead."
I had a heated argument with my partner. He left when I started crying.	"I feel like people don't understand me, so I need to avoid interacting with anyone. I'll just go to bed."	Encouraged me to avoid the issue and socially isolate by going to bed midday.	"My trauma voice is trying to help me deal with not feeling understood by telling me to avoid the issue with my partner and isolate by going to bed. I'll call a friend instead."

Trauma Voice and Response Chart

Event or situation Who? What? Where? When?	Trauma voice thought What was going through your mind?	Trauma response How did the trauma voice try to help you to cope?	Alternative behaviors What could you say and do to cope instead?

Reflect

Which alternative behavior do you believe would be the most helpful to counteract your trauma voice? Why? Were you able to better identify the trauma voice?

_____

_____

_____

_____

_____

_____

I'm feeling a sense of fear and panic.	**STOP**
I'm feeling intense rage toward myself and others.	**STOP**
I'm feeling hopeless and worse than I did before.	**STOP**
I'm feeling uncomfortable and anxious.	**GROUNDING**
I'm feeling some uneasiness, but overall okay.	**CONTINUE**

Finding Helpful Ways of Coping

Coping strategies are necessary for survival. If you didn't use coping strategies, you would probably feel even more overwhelmed. Coping strategies help you set boundaries and regulate what you can and cannot do. Some coping strategies, such as excessive drinking or substance use, can feel helpful in the short term but are unhelpful and self-destructive in the long term. If these coping strategies are used regularly and you're not aware of where they're coming from, you may develop patterns of behavior that can affect your mood, ability to have positive interpersonal relationships, and create further stress in your life.

Remember, your trauma voice may have instructed you to do things without you realizing there was an underlying need behind it. For example, if your trauma voice has directed you to isolate in response to feeling misunderstood, the underlying need was likely a need for validation, yet you coped by avoiding others. Once you understand what need these strategies are meeting, you can begin to make changes and use more helpful ways of coping.

Exploring Your Unmet Needs

It was mentioned in chapter 1 that childhood trauma, specifically sexual abuse, may lead to schema development, which is a negative core belief that you may hold about yourself or others. Considering the fact that you felt unsafe and possibly experienced abuse from the caregivers who were supposed to nurture and protect you, you may have developed a *mistrust schema*, leaving you feeling that you cannot trust others. Additionally, you may have felt invalidated if you reported the abuse to a family member or friend and did not receive a supportive response or were not believed. This may have led you to have an unmet need for love and acceptance.

As a result of the schemas you developed throughout your childhood, you may have difficulty reacting to situations in your adult life and may engage in behaviors intended to satisfy unmet needs in order to cope (Tanasugarn 2022). It's important to recognize that schemas operate on an unconscious level. Therefore, schemas that are unhelpful and even restricting—such as self-sacrificing thoughts like "I'll ignore what I want because I want to make them happy"—may seem right to you because they are familiar to how you felt as a child. Even decades after a traumatic event, you may still be experiencing unmet emotional needs.

In addition, since your emotional development may have been stunted in childhood, these unmet needs may have resulted in psychological and interpersonal difficulties as you grew into adulthood. Even so, you might not be aware of what that need is or why you respond to certain situations in a particular manner.

Let's explore four unmet needs commonly associated with childhood sexual abuse: *control, security, approval,* and *validation.* Discovering your unmet needs will help you be able to validate how you survived even in terrifying or unstable circumstances—which will ultimately enable you to heal and honor your lived experience.

CONTROL

As a survivor of sexual abuse, you had no control over what was happening to you. Do you feel a constant need to control your environment now? This need is entirely understandable given that you lacked that control when you were being traumatized. It makes sense that you may fear losing control now. However, a need for control can result in unhelpful and compulsive behaviors, such as binge eating or substance abuse.

In what ways does the need for control show up for you?

_____

_____

_____

_____

SECURITY

In order to feel secure, you must perceive that you are safe and protected from emotional, sexual, and physical harm. As a survivor, you grew up in an environment that felt unsafe and without protection. As a result of not being able to meet your security needs, you may seek out relationships with partners who can fulfill the role of protector for you (Brenner 2019). Given that you were not provided with adequate protection as a child, this too makes sense.

However, it's likely that your desire for a partner who will act as a protector will also trigger a fear of losing your protector. You may, therefore, fear abandonment and respond to this fear by clinging to the person.

Have you ever been terrified of losing someone you considered your protector and supporter? If so, how did you attempt to cope with the fear?

_____

_____

_____

_____

APPROVAL AND VALIDATION

Children naturally seek approval from their parents or caregivers. If your caregivers or parents were often critical or detached, it is likely that you did not receive the approval you needed. Throughout your life, you may have felt a growing need to seek approval and recognition from friends, teachers, employers, and partners. To gain approval and validation, you may have overcompensated by trying to please other people. To please everyone around you, you may have learned to ignore your own feelings and thoughts—and fear failure. Emotionally, this can be draining. It's likely, if this statement resonates with you, that you have consistently strived to accomplish more or do better to receive approval and validation. Having a constant need to be better can cause stress, intrusive thoughts, and symptoms of anxiety and depression.

Validation is similar to approval, however those seeking validation also wish to be recognized and praised. One way some people seek validation is through the use of social media. To be clear, taking and posting pictures of yourself does not necessarily imply a desire for validation. But if you are frequently posting multiple pictures of yourself in the hope of receiving positive comments and likes, it may indicate that you're using social media to feel validated.

In what ways does the need for approval and validation show up for you?

_____

_____

_____

_____

Unhelpful Coping Strategies

As a way of dealing with painful thoughts and feelings associated with your unmet needs, you may use a number of unhelpful coping strategies. Having explored your unmet needs, you can identify the unhelpful strategies you engage in. Take a look at the list below. Circle any unhelpful coping strategies that reflect your tendencies. Add any unhelpful or harmful strategies you use that are missing from this list.

Common Unhelpful Coping Strategies

Perfectionism	Sleeping excessively	People pleasing
Promiscuity	Not sleeping	Dependence on others
Avoiding sex	Hypervigilance	Need for control
Substance use	Workaholism	Avoidance of issues
Isolation	Self-harm	Minimizing feelings
Procrastination	Daydreaming	Excessive exercising
Self-blame	Binge eating	Thrill seeking or risky behaviors
Undereating	Restricting food	Impulsive spending

Now, let's identify the coping strategy your trauma voice instructs you to use, the underlying unmet need that motivates this coping strategy, and an alternative strategy for meeting that need. This exercise is inspired by Davis (1990, 158–160).

To start, look at the strategies you circled in the previous list. Then, refer to the Common Helpful Coping Strategies chart in the beginning of this chapter. Use that chart to determine the type of strategy most beneficial for meeting your needs in an alternative manner. Notice in the example provided that the underlying needs are in **bold**.

Since it may be challenging to distinguish between your trauma voice and your own rational thoughts, take your time with the following exercise. If you get stuck, ask someone on your Support System List (in the Introduction) for recommendations. The example below is based on the unmet need of approval. Refer to what you stated was your unmet need, identify the behavior meeting this need, and pick an alternative coping strategy that may help you meet that need.

Unmet Need #1: Need for Approval

Behavior meeting this need (trauma response):

Trying to be perfect in everything I do and feeling like a failure if I don't do something perfectly.

The unmet needs driving this strategy:

1. When I do well on a task, I feel accomplished and worthy of success.

2. Being the best parent or partner I can be allows me to feel worthy of love.

3. If I do things well, I'll get approval or validation from my family, friends, and employer.

4. I gain a sense of control by controlling things around me, which reduces my fear of losing control.

The helpful ways I can meet these needs would be to:

1. Recognize that perfection does not equate to doing everything correctly.

2. Accept and appreciate my accomplishments, which will provide me with the approval and validation I desire.

3. Take pride in myself.

4. Encourage myself to not push myself to be the best I can be—and instead appreciate the person that I show up to be that day.

5. Practice deep breathing or a mindfulness exercise when I fear losing control.

Unmet Need #1: _____

Behavior meeting this need (trauma response):

_____

_____

The unmet needs driving this strategy:

1. _____

2. _____

3. _____

4. _____

5. _____

The helpful ways I can meet these needs would be to:

1. _____

2. _____

3. _____

4. _____

5. _____

Unmet Need #2: _____

Behavior meeting this need (trauma response):

_____

_____

The unmet needs driving this strategy:

1. _____

2. _____

3. _____

4. _____

5. _____

The helpful ways I can meet these needs would be to:

1. _____

2. _____

3. _____

4. _____

5. _____

Unmet Need #3: _____

Behavior meeting this need (trauma response):

_____

_____

The unmet needs driving this strategy:

1. _____

2. _____

3. _____

4. _____

5. _____

The helpful ways I can meet these needs would be to:

1. _____

2. _____

3. _____

4. _____

5. _____

During the next week, see if you can identify any other coping strategies you are using. Use a separate piece of paper or a journal to repeat the exercise several more times. This is all part of the healing process. If you come up with an expanded list of helpful coping strategies, return to the last question on any of the Tying It All Together pages and answer that question again to see if your thoughts and feelings have changed on how to practice helpful ways to take care of yourself.

I'm feeling a sense of fear and panic.	STOP
I'm feeling intense rage toward myself and others.	STOP
I'm feeling hopeless and worse than I did before.	STOP
I'm feeling uncomfortable and anxious.	GROUNDING
I'm feeling some uneasiness, but overall okay.	CONTINUE

Self-Soothing: How It Can Help You

The trauma voice can create physical discomfort and negative thoughts and feelings. An emotion regulation strategy known as *self-soothing* can help reduce this discomfort.

It may come naturally to you to soothe others when they are upset, but you may have difficulty regulating your emotions when you're triggered. As a result of this difficulty, your interpersonal relationships may be strained, or you may use common unhelpful coping strategies, such as reaching for alcohol, socially isolating, binge watching a series, or overeating. As highlighted in previous sections, these strategies may be effective in the short term but don't serve you in the long term.

In certain circumstances, reaching out to someone who is on your Support System List can provide the reassurance you need to minimize stress. You may, however, have moments when you're unable to reach out for support, in which case self-soothing skills may prove useful. It can be beneficial to practice self-soothing techniques when you're not upset, so you can regulate your emotions more effectively when you are triggered (McKay and West 2016).

Self-Soothing Toolbox

As part of the next exercise, you'll put together a personal toolbox to help you explore self-soothing skills. Your self-soothing toolbox can comprise both objects and activities—anything that will help you feel more relaxed and reduce symptoms of anxiety or low mood. If you'd like to dedicate a physical container for your toolbox, consider a box, bag, or jar in which to store the objects. You'll be asked to consider calming objects and activities that involve one or more of the five senses.

Each chart that follows provides examples of what may be calming. As you review each chart, write down the items you'd like to include in your self-soothing toolbox. Be as specific as possible.

Sight. There is no doubt that our sense of sight has a significant impact on our emotions, both positive and negative. For example, natural environments are known to reduce stress and to increase positive mood (Bratman, Hamilton, and Daily 2012). As you read the examples, consider what brings you calmness or happiness. Knowing which images evoke happiness or calmness will enable you to use them when you're in distress.

Sight
• Look at things that are soothing to the eye, such as a candle burning, soft lights, or an inspirational quote.
• Browse through pictures of loved ones. Pets, friends, partners, or family members are good subjects.
• Spend some time outside observing the scenery around you. Take in the flowers, trees, a body of water, a park, the sky. You may wish to take a picture of this place so that you'll still have visual access to it if you're unable to go outside.
• Engage in a mindful visual activity, such as coloring, painting, or drawing.

The following **sight** items will help me practice self-soothing, and I'll include them in my self-soothing toolbox:

1. _____

2. _____

3. _____

Sound. A soothing sound can have a powerful effect on the body. After acute stress exposure, relaxing music can reduce anxiety, depression, and increase positive affect (de la Torre-Luque, Díaz-Piedra, and Buela-Casal 2017). Identify the types of relaxing music you enjoy and create a playlist. Store this playlist wherever it is most accessible when you wish to relax and calm down.

Sound
• Listen to relaxation or meditation music through YouTube audio or apps such as Calm and Headspace.
• Play a sound machine that emanates the sounds of water, birds, rain, or waves. Or play them on YouTube or other apps.
• Listen to the sounds of a body of water such as a waterfall, stream, or ocean while closing your eyes.
• Take a moment to sit in silence with your eyes closed and notice the sounds you hear around you. You may hear a clock ticking, the hum of your heater, the sounds of cars passing outside, or a distant wind chime.

The following **sound** items will help me practice self-soothing, and I'll include them in my self-soothing toolbox:

1. _____

2. _____

3. _____

Taste. Enjoyable activities such as cooking and eating a delicious meal can provide a great source of stress relief. Chefs often describe how preparing food requires them to be mindful of selecting the right ingredients. They also describe how food is connected to their fond memories or relationships, providing them with feelings of completeness and satisfaction. Whatever your culinary expertise, cooking with others can provide a sense of calm and connection that may be helpful in reducing stress.

In addition, by observing the flavors and textures on your tongue, you may be able to relax as you savor the chosen treat. As you review the examples, consider the items you may enjoy tasting; plan ahead so you can have them on hand when needed.

Taste
• Sip a steaming cup of coffee or tea. Calming teas include mint, chamomile, lavender, rose, and matcha.
• Keep a supply of strong mints, chocolate, chewing gum, or sour sweets on hand in case of distress.
• Enjoy your favorite meal by preparing or eating it. Be sure to savor all the flavors by eating it slowly and mindfully.
• Indulge in your favorite treat by focusing on all five senses to enhance the experience of it. For example, start by smelling it, then notice its features, then explore its textures on your tongue, and finally, listen to the sounds it makes as you bite down.

The following **taste** items will help me practice self-soothing, and I'll include them in my self-soothing toolbox:

1. _____

2. _____

3. _____

Smell. Among all senses, smell is most closely associated with memory. The best way to find out which smells are relaxing for you or remind you of a pleasant memory is to experiment with various scents. If you know which smells promote a calm state of mind, you can use these when you need them following a triggering situation.

Smell
• Take a moment to notice the smell in your favorite restaurant or coffee shop.
• Wear essential oils, scented body sprays or lotions, or perfumes that make you feel cheerful or assertive.
• Use incense or a candle with your favorite scent.
• Spend time outdoors smelling the flowers and trees, or purchase flowers for your home.

The following **smell** items will help me practice self-soothing, and I'll include them in my self-soothing toolbox:

1. _____

2. _____

3. _____

Touch. Whenever we experience strong emotions, our bodies automatically prepare reflective responses that may result in tension. These muscles can be relaxed by certain exercises and massages. The more you become aware of the textures and modes of touch that soothe you, the more you'll be prepared to use these strategies to feel calm when experiencing strong emotions. The first example of self-soothing touch is recommended by Dreisoerner et al. (2021).

Touch
• Place your right hand over your heart and your left hand over your stomach while paying attention to your breath rising and falling.
• Keep a stress ball or a squishy ball on hand for when you feel upset.
• Enjoy a hot bath and feel the warmth on your skin.
• Gently rub a pet, a cozy blanket, or a piece of clothing that feels very soft in your hands.
• Keep a piece of soft fabric in your pocket to touch when you're upset. A microfiber cloth used for cleaning eyeglasses works well.

The following **touch** items will help me practice self-soothing, and I'll include them in my self-soothing toolbox:

1. _____

2. _____

3. _____

Over the next week or two, use several self-soothing items from your toolbox. Once you get a feel for which self-soothing items provide you with the greatest level of comfort, continue to use these items on a regular basis.

Tying It All Together

Everyone needs to utilize coping strategies to deal with life stressors. As a survivor, you've depended on a variety of coping strategies. You needed to do this to withstand abusive events that challenged your feeling of safety. This can explain how you developed a trauma voice and why you may react negatively when certain memories or triggers arise. Unfortunately, unhelpful coping strategies may cause further difficulties for you.

Fortunately, there are effective coping strategies that can help you meet your unmet needs. Self-soothing is one such strategy, and it's also an excellent method of acknowledging and managing intense emotions. If you practice nurturing yourself during times of distress, you can reduce their intensity and achieve a sense of calm.

I hope this chapter has helped you learn the following:

- The trauma voice is derived from the brain reacting to stress and trauma, and this voice helped you survive.

- It's not your fault that persistent thoughts might lead you to use unhelpful coping strategies.

- Yet, you may feel uncomfortable challenging or accepting your thinking because you've become accustomed to believing those thoughts are your own rational thoughts when they are simply a way for your mind to cope.

- Accepting where you are enhances your awareness of your trauma voice and assists you in identifying when it is speaking, allowing you to take actions (for example, self-soothing, seeking support, spending time outdoors) that are more aligned with who you want to be.

- By recognizing the coping strategies you are using, you can begin to manage triggering thoughts and feelings by learning alternative coping behaviors.

It's difficult to focus on nurturing yourself when you're in a constant state of survival. The more you become aware of your automatic responses, the more likely you can develop and practice coping skills that nurture yourself. The next chapter will help you identify self-care goals, examine the impact abuse may have had on your ability to trust yourself, and learn how to be self-compassionate while focusing on your strengths and accomplishments.

Please consider the following questions to reflect on your present feelings, needs, and goals regarding the voice that helped you survive and how you coped with it:

By identifying my ways of coping and my trauma voice, what did I learn about my trauma voice?

_____

_____

_____

_____

Can I practice using the coping strategies I came up with, and if so, are they reasonable alternatives?

_____

_____

_____

_____

What goals would I like to set for this week to practice identifying my trauma voice and establishing helpful ways of coping?

_____

_____

_____

_____

What exercises were too difficult for me to do that I would like to return to later? What is getting in the way of me being able to work through this area?

_____

_____

_____

_____

What do I need to do to take care of myself and ensure that I'm practicing self-care (for example, spend time outdoors, meditate, take a break from this workbook)?

_____

_____

_____

_____

On a scale of 1 to 10, rate your level of hope both *before* you began this chapter and *currently*.	
1 = feeling completely hopeless	Before the chapter _____
10 = feeling extremely hopeful	After the chapter _____

CHAPTER 4

Nurturing, Trusting, and Loving Yourself

"Owning our story and loving ourselves through that process is the bravest thing that we'll ever do."

—Brené Brown

As we go through our busy lives, we often get caught up in what we need to get done instead of focusing on what we need to do to take care of ourselves. This is true for many people. However, as a survivor, learning how to provide self-care is monumentally important for the healing process.

You may be unable to trust yourself or others as a result of your experience of childhood sexual abuse (Davis 1990; Ferrajão and Elklit 2020). Some survivors are exposed to abuse by those that should be responsible for teaching a child that the world is safe and that they can trust their needs to be met. When you were abused, you may not have received the type of nurturing and support that encourages self-acceptance. The fact that you did not receive this support as a child may make it difficult for you to provide love and care for yourself as an adult, but it is something you can learn.

The process of healing can create intense feelings, so it's important that you take it slow, rest, and be gentle with yourself. Adding more stress into your life is not the goal of healing. The goal is for you to accept where you are and learn strategies for restoring your hope that you will heal and be exactly as you would like to be.

As a child, you may have tried to nurture yourself in a harmful way, such as partaking in risky behaviors. You may already know the best way to nurture yourself now, but feelings of sadness and shame are preventing you from feeling that you deserve to be nurtured. On the other hand, you may believe that you only need nurturing when you're sick or your family is experiencing a stressful event. These moments may force you to stop, rest, and take care of yourself, but taking care of your needs should be part of your daily routine.

To develop a daily self-care regimen, it's helpful to brainstorm all the ways to nurture yourself. On the lines below, devise a list of activities that are enjoyable, provide relaxation, enhance your sense of well-being and happiness, and feel nurturing. Then, circle three that you're confident about being able to use daily.

Here are some examples:

- "I'll spend time outdoors."

- "I'll call an old friend to reconnect."

- "I'll express my feelings through art, such as listening to music, painting, or drawing."

- "I'll take a long bath."

- "I'll get a new haircut or style."

- "I'll practice yoga or any exercise program that I enjoy."

1. _____

2. _____

3. _____

4. _____

5. _____

6. _____

7. _____

Setting Goals for Self-Care

Let's continue to evaluate how well you've been nurturing yourself. Refer to the self-care list you just made and locate the three options you circled. List them in the chart that follows. Then, ask yourself the following questions to complete the chart:

- "How often have I been doing this?" (for example, daily, several times a week, once a year)

- "How can I increase or improve this type of nurturing?" (for example, by trying to do this every day)

Then create a goal for the week that would allow you to practice self-care:

- "My weekly goal will be…" (for example, to spend time outdoors before work and once in the evening)

Ways to Nurture Myself

Ways I can nurture myself	How often I'm doing this	How I can improve nurturing myself	My weekly goal

At the end of the week, come back to this exercise to reflect and evaluate your progress.

This week I was able to nurture myself by: _____

_____

_____

My goal for next week is to nurture myself by: _____

_____

_____

I'm feeling a sense of fear and panic.		**STOP**
I'm feeling intense rage toward myself and others.		**STOP**
I'm feeling hopeless and worse than I did before.		**STOP**
I'm feeling uncomfortable and anxious.		**GROUNDING**
I'm feeling some uneasiness, but overall okay.		**CONTINUE**

CHeCK In

Trusting Yourself

You may doubt whether what you're feeling and thinking is valid, and, as a result, you may distrust your own intuition. The reason for this is that childhood abuse has a significant impact on an individual's ability to trust themselves and others (Davis 1990; Ferrajão and Elklit 2020). As a child, you naturally trusted those who provided care for you. When the environment was unsafe, as in the case of sexual abuse, you may have stopped trusting and started to question your own perceptions and feelings. Childhood sexual abuse placed you in a position to feel powerless and to doubt your decision to trust those who had hurt you.

It's also important to understand the mixed messages you may have received when the abuse was taking place. Many survivors report being confused and internalizing statements their abusers made (Karakurt and Silver 2014; Levenkron and Levenkron 2007). Abusers may distort reality by stating, "You have to do this, and you can't tell your mother because she will be upset with you" or "You were bad last week, and if you tell, then everyone will think you deserved it."

Since children typically believe what adults say, these statements can become an abused child's new reality. The cultural factors in your family may have also made it difficult for you to trust yourself, especially if you felt that disclosing the abuse would have a negative impact on your family. Consequently, you may have been concerned that if you reported the incident, the police would come and your family would blame you for the disruption. As a result of this fear, you may have put the needs of others ahead of your own sense of security. This is similar to the fawning response of pleasing others that we discussed in previous chapters.

If you did not learn to trust your feelings and intuitions as a child, you can learn how to do so today by evaluating internalized messages that may still be lingering and resolve them. Remember, an internalized message may be anything that was said to you to coerce you into silence or obedience. As a child, you may have viewed these statements as "true" statements. This is your opportunity to release internalized messages and create a more realistic picture of who you are.

In the next exercise, you'll examine whether any internalized messages you may still be carrying as a result of messages you heard as a child have caused you to experience self-hatred.

1. In the first column, circle the statements that best represent something you may have been told as a child. Some of these may not apply to you. Write down specific statements not listed that are relevant to you.

2. In the middle column are beliefs you might have developed from hearing these statements. These are beliefs that were taught to you. Identify the belief that matches what you circled. If nothing matches, write down what you were taught. Then, draw a line between the statement and the resulting belief.

3. In the third column, list all the things you still think or feel about yourself. By looking at all three lists, see if you can identify if this current feeling or thought may be stemming from an internalized message.

Internalized Messages

When I was a child, I was told...	The abuse taught me that...	I still believe that...
"You must do this, and if you tell your parents, you'll upset them."	I have to do things I don't want to do in order to keep people from being upset with me.	If I do things to keep people happy, I can prevent them from being upset with me.
"No one will ever love you."	I am unlovable.	
"You're bad, and if you were good, this wouldn't be happening to you."	I'm unworthy of love.	
"You're worthless and only good for sex."	It's my fault that bad things happen to me.	

When I was a child, I was told...	The abuse taught me that...	I still believe that...
"You're a liar, so if you tell, no one will believe you."	I don't deserve anything better than this.	
"Stop crying! You deserve to be hurt!"	Expression of emotion is bad.	
"You're ugly, and no one will want you if I don't teach you these things."	Pleasing a person is more important than what I feel.	
"It's normal for little children to please adults."	My word has no value, and it's better just to keep what I think and feel to myself.	

Simply identifying negative messages that you may have internalized will not erase the negative effect these messages may have had on your ability to trust yourself. But it's a step in the direction of learning how to minimize the impact of these messages on your life. When you can see where the bad feelings about yourself are coming from, you can begin to have compassion for yourself and realize that these feelings are not true. It will take time and practice to identify and determine the source of these thoughts. By doing this exercise for several weeks, you will slowly make steps toward healing and trusting yourself.

Reflect

If you noticed internalized messages that you may be still holding, reflect on what came up for you. What thoughts, feelings, or sensations showed up?

_____

_____

_____

_____

_____

If you're still holding an internalized message, how might you practice self-compassion when these thoughts and feelings arise? If so, what would you tell yourself now?

_____

_____

_____

_____

_____

I'm feeling a sense of fear and panic.	**STOP**
I'm feeling intense rage toward myself and others.	**STOP**
I'm feeling hopeless and worse than I did before.	**STOP**
I'm feeling uncomfortable and anxious.	**GROUNDING**
I'm feeling some uneasiness, but overall okay.	**CONTINUE**

Replacing Negative Thoughts with Affirmations

One way you can start reducing the impact of negative thoughts is by replacing them with positive affirmations about yourself. Essentially, an *affirmation* is a positive statement of truth that declares your strengths in a powerful and meaningful manner. When you repeat them often, and believe in them, you start to make positive changes and replace the negative thoughts that were once in your mind.

Although you might consider these statements as simply "wishful thinking," saying them is a proven-effective way to exercise your mind and reprogram persistent thinking patterns so that, over time, you begin to think and act differently. Remember that, as a child, you were told lies designed to coerce, control, and keep you silent. The practice of stating affirmations can eliminate those lies.

Sometimes, it can be a challenge to think positively about yourself, especially if early programming interfered with your ability to do so. If that is the case, ask one or two people on your Support System List (in the Introduction) what positive qualities they see in you. Then use those statements to create your affirmations in the next exercise.

1. On the following lines, write down several statements that affirm your truest, deepest, most authentic self. You can use the examples as a guide.

    "I'm a survivor with an immense amount of strength and determination."

    "I'm lovable and I deserve respect."

    "I'm beautiful inside and out, and I'm a catch for any person worthy of my trust."

    _____

    _____

    _____

    _____

    _____

    _____

    _____

2. Next, transfer one affirmation to a blank piece of paper. Draw or sketch around the words to create a visualization of what this affirmation may mean to you. You can also paste magazine pictures on the page that reflect what the statement means to you.

3. Repeat this process for at least two more affirmations or as many as you would like.

4. Then, post your affirmation artwork on a wall. Having this visual will help remind you of the importance of your affirmations.

5. Next, using the worksheet that follows, set a goal for how often, when, and where you will practice saying these affirmations.

6. Practice for one month and then return to this exercise to determine which affirmations, if any, created a positive belief in yourself.

Weekly Affirmation Goals

Week 1: This week, my affirmation is _____

_____ .

I'll state my affirmation _____ times a _____ (day, week). I can practice it at _____

(home, work) and/or while I am _____

(spending time outdoors, doing chores, exercising).

Week 2: This week, my affirmation is _____

_____ .

I'll state my affirmation _____ times a _____ (day, week). I can practice it at _____

(home, work) and/or while I am _____

(spending time outdoors, doing chores, exercising).

Week 3: This week, my affirmation is _____

_____ .

I'll state my affirmation _____ times a _____ (day, week). I can practice it at _____ (home, work) and/or while I am _____

(spending time outdoors, doing chores, exercising).

Week 4: This week, my affirmation is _____

_____ .

I'll state my affirmation _____ times a _____ (day, week). I can practice it at _____

(home, work) and/or while I am _____

(spending time outdoors, doing chores, exercising).

It can be uncomfortable to tell yourself things you don't necessarily believe, but it is this type of reprogramming that can change how we think over time. And once that occurs, you will act differently, especially toward yourself. Once you've practiced for a month, you'll find that what once felt awkward will now feel natural and easy.

After one month of practicing your affirmations, complete the following sentence:

The affirmations that created acceptance or change, and that I now believe about myself, are:

_____

_____

_____

_____

_____

_____

Listening to Your Inner Voice

There is an *inner voice* within each of us. Although the inner voice is not an actual voice that you hear, it's the inner mechanism that is derived of intuition, feelings, instincts, and thoughts that can guide your decision-making process. An example of this voice may be a gut instinct that tells you when something might be dangerous or not in your best interest. In essence, this voice guides you to act. By listening to your inner voice, you can decide what to do in these situations.

For example, you are hiking and the path becomes narrow and inclines into an area that you can't see; your inner voice may sense danger, so you decide to turn back. Or, you're at a party and you meet someone new, but shortly into the encounter you recognize signs that the person appears to have little regard for others by criticizing them; you decide to excuse yourself and not pursue that relationship further.

Many people have a hard time listening to this voice, especially those who struggle with trusting their gut feelings and thoughts. For those who have experienced childhood sexual abuse, listening to their inner voice can be quite challenging, because their inner voice was silenced and replaced with mixed messages from their abuser. When you were abused, you had to ignore your gut feelings and thoughts to get through the abuse. Learning to listen to your inner voice means learning how to trust what your mind and body are telling you.

It's likely that you're now wondering what the difference is between your trauma voice and your inner voice. As noted in chapter 3, your trauma voice is the voice of survival, frequently triggered by stress or critical thoughts about yourself or others. The trauma voice may also function as a coping mechanism, urging you to act to alleviate discomfort or pain. Your inner voice, on the other hand, guides you or warns you of danger to assist you in making a decision. Let's look at the chart for comparison.

Difference Between Your Trauma Voice and Inner Voice

Trauma voice	Inner voice
• Uses black and white thinking	• Recognizes complexity and gray areas
• Focuses on problems	• Focuses on solutions
• Doesn't recognize or celebrate accomplishments	• Celebrates small victories or progress
• Uses shame, guilt, and fear to motivate you to act	• Uses a gut feeling, desire, or compassion to motivate you to act
• Focuses on what is lacking or never enough	• Focuses on what is possible or feels right

By practicing how to listen to your inner voice, you're in essence breaking the silence that was part of your trauma experience and taking back your voice. This can be intimidating yet empowering. Learning how your inner voice communicates with you will take time. The good news is that there are things you can do now to prepare yourself to be a better receiver. For instance, you can notice when you have an urge to use a schema coping behavior and then come up with an alternative way to respond *as if* you were listening to the wisdom of your inner voice. Using the example as a guide, fill out the form with what feels possible for you.

Example:

When I am about to make an unhealthy decision, I sometimes feel indecisive and have the sense that something is wrong. I usually ignore it. When this happens, I often feel a headache coming on and mentally drained.

When I am about to make an unhealthy decision, I sometimes feel _____ and have the sense

that _____. I usually _____ (ignore, listen) to it. When this happens, I

often feel _____

(physical or mental sensation).

When I know something is right for me, I usually feel _____ and have the sense that

_____. I usually _____ (ignore, listen) to it. When this happens, I

often feel _____

(physical or mental sensation).

When I am in danger or I know something isn't quite right, I often experience sensations of _____

_____ and I start _____. When this happens, I

often recall _____

_____.

Circle the clause that most often applies to you: My *first instinct is to…*

- Ignore my inner voice.

- Listen to my inner voice.

- Pretend my inner voice isn't there.

Compare the times when you know something is right for you to the times when you know a decision may be unhealthy or dangerous. Based on your answers above, think about how your mind and body are trying to communicate to you. Do you see an internal difference between when you know something is right for you versus when you feel as if something may not be right for you? If not, that is okay; come back to this when you can and try again. If so, what is different about the times you listen to your inner voice and the times you don't?

_____

_____

_____

_____

_____

_____

_____

I'm feeling a sense of fear and panic.	**STOP**
I'm feeling intense rage toward myself and others.	**STOP**
I'm feeling hopeless and worse than I did before.	**STOP**
I'm feeling uncomfortable and anxious.	**GROUNDING**
I'm feeling some uneasiness, but overall okay.	**CONTINUE**

Check In

Loving Yourself

This workbook has been leading to this very important part of healing: loving yourself. It's an essential component of healing from childhood sexual abuse. Self-love comes in many forms, and you've already learned that part of loving yourself starts with awareness of where you are in this journey. By practicing self-acceptance, listening to your inner voice, affirming your strengths, and setting goals that can help you explore your passions and talents, you'll establish a love for yourself that you may or may not have known was there all along.

To truly love ourselves, we must be able to celebrate our accomplishments fully without minimizing them. Survivors often minimize the accomplishments they have made, partly due to the programming done in childhood. As you've learned, such programming can include internalized messages, such as "Nothing I do is good enough" or "I'm not special, and anyone can do what I've done."

The first thing you can acknowledge is that your survival is an enormous accomplishment that takes courage, strength, and resilience. Be proud of that! Own the fact that you're here today because of who you are—a strong person who fought to make it.

Acknowledging and Celebrating Your Accomplishments

You can start acknowledging your accomplishments by making a list of the things you have accomplished so far in your life. This may not be an easy task if you've focused more on survival than honoring your accomplishments. If this is the case for you, consider:

- Achievements at school and work

- All the times you've recognized schema coping behaviors and changed them

- Examples of your parenting or relationship style that is different than what was modeled for you

Include things from your growing-up years as well as accomplishments you've had in adulthood. For instance, "I provided my own financial and emotional support through the process of obtaining a college degree even though I spent my childhood feeling not good enough" or "I sought therapy for depression and stopped cutting" or "I told my mom that her boyfriend sexually abused me."

My Accomplishments

_____

_____

_____

_____

_____

_____

_____

_____

_____

_____

_____

_____

_____

Have you recognized these accomplishments in the past? It's likely that you've minimized your accomplishments and not given yourself permission to be proud of yourself for the things you've accomplished. Let's change that now by creating a list of ways to honor yourself and recognize past—and future—accomplishments. When you think of new ideas, add them to your list. Any time you accomplish something, consider one of these celebration ideas.

Ways to Celebrate My Accomplishments

_____

_____

_____

_____

_____

_____

_____

_____

_____

_____

_____

_____

What Is Self-Compassion?

We can demonstrate self-compassion by displaying love, understanding, and acceptance of ourselves. As a survivor, you may find it difficult to extend the same compassion toward yourself that you do to others. The reason for this may be related to internalized messages you accepted as truth. It may be helpful to first understand what compassion feels like.

A researcher who studies self-compassion, Kristin Neff (2023) defines *compassion* as the recognition of suffering in others, the heartfelt response you have to their suffering, and the realization that such suffering is a part of the shared experience of humanity. Further, Neff defines *self-compassion* as the ability to act the same way toward yourself when you observe something you dislike about yourself, fail, or are experiencing difficulties. In such challenging situations, self-compassion means acknowledging difficulties and comforting yourself.

The steps you take may be similar to what you would do for a friend who is experiencing the same problem, such as practicing kindness in the face of uncomfortable and disturbing emotions. This means honoring and accepting that you're human and make mistakes. It is by honoring this aspect of yourself that you can be more understanding toward yourself in the face of difficulties rather than direct your frustration and stress inward.

You may be wondering how you can accomplish this when you feel overwhelmed by your emotions. You can start by being willing to observe negative emotions and thoughts mindfully without trying to avoid them. In truth, it's impossible to be self-compassionate while ignoring your feelings. You can discover how to acknowledge, honor, and accept your thoughts and feelings without acting on the urge to avoid them by practicing mindfulness similar to the Mindful Acceptance Meditation, in chapter 2.

The Benefits of Self-Compassion

Self-compassion contributes to increased psychological well-being. As a result of the trauma, survivors often experience symptoms of anxiety, depression, rumination, and fear of failure. Through self-compassion, these symptoms can be reduced; in their place come feelings of connection, happiness, and optimism (Neff 2009). It's important to note that when you practice self-compassion, you will not belittle yourself when you don't succeed; rather, you'll celebrate your accomplishments and admit your mistakes. In contrast to those seeking approval or validation, self-compassionate individuals seek to learn and grow for intrinsic reasons.

A healthy lifestyle, enriched relationships, and a sense of general well-being can be achieved through nurturing and loving yourself. The ability to be self-compassionate will enable you to acknowledge when you're suffering and to be kind to yourself during these times, decreasing the anxiety and depression that can accompany suffering.

Incorporating Self-Compassion into Your Daily Life

Enhancing your ability to be self-compassionate will take time. If you practice the exercises that follow, you may find it strange at first. However, be patient. The possible results can outweigh any discomfort you may feel.

A DAILY COMPLIMENT

This exercise assists you in countering your trauma voice through identifying the positive aspects of yourself and reframing any self-critical thoughts. It can be used at any time of the day. If you have difficulty thinking of a positive thing about yourself, ask someone on your Support System List what they appreciate about you. You'll need a pack of sticky notes for this exercise.

1. At least once per day, write something you appreciate, admire, or respect about yourself on a sticky note.

2. Place this note where you'll see it, for example, on the bathroom mirror or refrigerator, or at your workstation.

3. Over the next twenty-four hours, read the note as often as you would like.

4. Create a new sticky note each day.

After a week of practice, think of something you don't appreciate, admire, or respect about yourself. Pause for a moment before writing this negative thought on a sticky note and instead ask yourself the following questions:

- How can I express kindness to myself right now?

- May I learn to accept myself as I am?

- How can I show myself compassion right now?

Reflect on the negative thought you just had. Notice if it was a self-critical thought. Ask yourself, "Are these words that I recall saying to myself over and over? If so, what are they?"

_____

_____

_____

_____

_____

Ask yourself, "Does this voice remind me of something someone in the past has said to me? If so, when was the first time I heard these words and who said them?

_____

_____

_____

_____

Now, try to soften your trauma voice with a compassionate statement. For instance, if your initial thought was "No matter how hard I try, I always mess things up," speak to your trauma voice by saying something like, "I know you feel frustrated and worried that you may not succeed, but you're causing more suffering. Can I allow my compassionate voice to speak now?" (Neff 2023).

If you have difficulty finding compassionate words to say, close your eyes and imagine what one of your supportive friends might say to you. For example, they may say to you (and you can say to yourself), "I know you feel overwhelmed and you would like to achieve this goal. Sometimes when we get overwhelmed and feel anxious, it can make us feel worse. I want you to be happy, so why don't you take a break, spend some time outdoors, so you feel less anxious? When you're ready, you can come back to this and work on it."

Now, open your eyes and say these words aloud while you write them on a sticky note. You may repeat this exercise as often as you wish. As challenging as this may seem at first, the key is to practice being kind to yourself, and eventually these statements will feel genuine and caring.

SELF-COMPASSION JOURNAL

Keeping a journal is a valuable method of expressing your feelings and can be beneficial to your mental and physical well-being (Neff 2023). If you keep a daily journal, you can record any self-critical thoughts you may be having or any unpleasant experiences you may have had. Perhaps when you were in an argument with your partner, you felt intense sadness and loneliness. Instead of expressing these feelings, you yelled at your partner, slammed the door, and left the house. When you left, the sadness and loneliness intensified, but you also experienced feelings of guilt. Journaling can help you sort out your emotions, thoughts, and behaviors.

Use the following examples and chart to start a flow of writing.

1. Bring your awareness to the emotions that arose during the event. Write about what you felt: anger, sadness, shame, fear, anxiety, and so on. As you write, speak from your compassionate voice, not your self-critical trauma voice. For example, "I was sad because my partner didn't

understand my point of view. I became frustrated, overreacted, and felt guilty for not telling my partner that the misunderstanding left me feeling lonely and misunderstood."

2. Using a gentle tone, write comforting and kind words to yourself to show yourself how much you care about your feelings. For example, "It's okay that you didn't express your feelings the way you would have liked. I understand how overwhelmed you were, especially when you felt isolated and lonely. You lost your composure, but maybe next time you can try acknowledging where this feeling is coming from and tell your partner exactly how you're feeling."

3. Use the following chart if you need help organizing your thoughts and emotions before journaling. Create a copy of this chart and keep it in your journal, or download a free copy at http://www .newharbinger.com/53790.

Self-Compassion Journal Log

Event	Description of what I felt in a compassionate tone:	Comforting and kind words that show how much I care about how I felt or am feeling now:

CELEBRATE THE SMALL WINS

The majority of your goals will not be achieved in one day, but recognizing your progress is important. Using this approach ensures that you'll experience more self-compassion and happiness than if you waited for a goal to be completed before feeling worthy of happiness. Recognizing your progress toward a goal activates your brain's reward center, which releases dopamine, the chemical that causes you to feel good.

Furthermore, if you feel good about each small win, you'll be motivated to keep moving forward until you reach your ultimate goal. You might find it challenging at first to find a small win to celebrate each day, but with some digging, you'll be able to identify the small accomplishments you make daily.

Review the list of examples of small wins, along with the suggestions for ways to celebrate these accomplishments. Over the next week, use these examples and suggestions if they resonate with you, or create your own. On the log provided, write down what you did each day to practice celebrating small wins. Then, rate your level of self-compassion on a scale of 0 (not self-compassionate) to 10 (very self-compassionate). If you would like additional copies of the log, download a free copy at http://www.newharbinger.com/53790.

Here are common examples of small wins worthy of celebration:

- I trusted my inner voice and used it to guide a decision.

- I used a mindfulness activity to help me cope with intense emotions.

- I stated a few words of kindness toward myself and meant it.

- I encouraged a friend, and I believe I can provide that same care toward myself.

- I completed an act of self-care.

- I practiced boundaries and said no.

- I expressed my feelings to myself.

- I expressed my feelings to someone I care about.

- I focused on my physical well-being by exercising or eating a nutritious meal.

- I observed the urge to avoid but neither judged nor acted on it.

- I asked for help when I needed it.

- I felt inspired to do an activity that I used to enjoy and have avoided.

- I noticed when my trauma voice was speaking.

- I recognized that I needed time for myself and took that time.

- I spent time outdoors.

- I used self-soothing to focus on using my senses.

Here are some possible ways to celebrate your small wins this week:

- Keep a record in my journal of all my daily small wins as a way to offer myself encouragement.

- Share my accomplishments with my friends, family, or colleagues.

- Treat myself by taking a long bath or baking and eating my favorite dessert.

- Engage in a self-care activity (for example, breathing technique, stretching, or meditation) immediately following the win.

- Validate my success to myself by saying something like, "I'm doing well, and I'm proud of myself."

- Take action to show kindness or gratitude toward another individual.

- Enjoy a moment at the park, zoo, art gallery, concert, or anywhere else that will stimulate my senses.

- Surprise myself with a gift (maybe that $25 hand lotion?).

Celebrating My Small Wins Log

Date	Small win I celebrated	Way I celebrated	Self-compassion rating (0 to 10)

Tying It All Together

Regardless of whether you received nurturing as a child or not, learning how to nurture yourself is a skill that takes time to develop. It is a crucial element of your healing process. As you learn to nurture yourself, you open yourself up to being able to begin trusting your own thoughts, feelings, and intuitions about what is best for you. With daily practice, you'll become more familiar with listening to your inner voice and trusting that the self-critical feelings and thoughts you may have about yourself were placed there from when you were a child trying to survive sexual abuse.

When you trust yourself, you'll pay attention to your instincts and the perceptions that may arise from them. Once you're in a place where nurturing and trusting yourself feels automatic and natural, you will establish a greater sense of self-love. This may be a slow process. You are unraveling the programming that was done when you were sexually abused, but with patience, being kind to yourself, and celebrating your accomplishments, self-love will naturally develop.

In the next chapter, we will explore what hope means to you and how enhancing hope in your life can help you achieve goals that align with your values. The following questions will help you assess your feelings and goals related to nurturing, trusting, and loving yourself:

What did I learn about nurturing myself, and in what ways will I continue to do this?

_____

_____

_____

_____

What did I learn about my inner voice? What commitments have I made about paying attention to my inner voice? What steps have I already taken to continue working toward listening to my inner voice?

_____

_____

_____

_____

What feelings did I have when I listed my accomplishments? What was hard about this for me? What have I done that I'm proud of and want to continually celebrate?

_____

_____

_____

_____

What positive aspects of myself do I now believe that I struggled to believe before?

_____

_____

_____

_____

What negative aspects of myself do I still believe and would like to continue to transform?

_____

_____

_____

_____

What do I need to do to take care of myself and ensure that I'm practicing self-care (for example, spend time outdoors, meditate, take a break from this workbook)?

_____

_____

_____

_____

_____

_____

_____

On a scale of 1 to 10, rate your level of hope both *before* you began this chapter and *currently*.

    1 = feeling completely hopeless

    10 = feeling extremely hopeful

Before the chapter _____

After the chapter _____

CHAPTER 5

Emergence of Hope

"Hope matters. Hope is a choice. Hope can be learned. Hope can be shared with others."

—Shane J. Lopez

Although *hope* can mean different things to different people, I define hope in this book as: the belief that change for the better is possible. For some people, hope comes in a spiritual form through the act of prayer. For others, hope comes from simply looking on the bright side and believing in the best outcome. Despite the different interpretations and presentations of hope, hope can mean the difference between hanging on and giving up.

You may not realize this yet, but you've already demonstrated the ability to have hope. You're here. You hung on through an abusive encounter and survived. You didn't give up. You have this book in your hands, which signals hope that things can be better. Hope means believing that healing is not only possible but that it's the direct result of action that you can take. Envisioning a better future motivates you to take the steps to make it happen.

When you experienced childhood sexual abuse, you couldn't control the situation nor could you make the abuse stop. That lack of control has a lot to do with why you may feel unsure about yourself and others. Hope is something you can control. You can make a conscious decision to heal and believe that, with hope, you'll receive the outcome you desire: a better life with fewer trauma responses, anxiety, and schemas.

Hope for the future can help you both heal and accept the areas in your life that may have been preventing you from achieving your goals. This may mean reflecting on painful memories of when you abandoned hope. As you learn how to transform your hopes into goals, explore your values, and align your actions with your values, you'll develop coping skills that will help you manage painful emotions.

Emergence of Hope Within You

In order to heal, you need to have hope. Developing hope for the future can promote your resiliency and healing. In turn, it can support a shift from repetitive negative thinking to a more positive outlook and more ease with establishing new goals for coping (Kaye-Tzadok and Davidson-Arad 2016). In practice, this is more difficult than it sounds. You may struggle to maintain a sense of hope because your abusive childhood left you feeling hopeless when the abuse continued (Davis 1990).

When you were being sexually abused, you might have thought, attempted, and hoped that if you did something specific then the abuse would stop. You might have thought, "If my stepmom thinks I'm a good person, then she will stop hurting me. I'll help around the house, so she will think I'm good." Or, "If I act out, my mom will know something is wrong. If she notices that something is wrong, I'll tell her, and she can make the babysitter stop touching me." Yet, if these attempts or thoughts did not produce the outcome you were hoping for, you were left feeling like it was pointless to hope for change. To survive, you may have needed to stop hoping for change.

It can be helpful to review the childhood hopes you had but never materialized, so you can understand why being hopeful takes more work for you. The next exercise will help you do that. Write down the hopes you had as a child, what happened instead, and the feelings or reactions that resulted. One example is provided. Note: if you find this exercise to be too painful or it stirs up feelings you would rather not relive, skip it and go to the next exercise.

My Childhood Hopes

My hopes as a child	Did my hope come true? (Yes or No)	What actually happened?	When my hopes were destroyed, I felt and reacted…
I hoped my mom would notice that me being quiet and withdrawn was not normal.	No	Family members labeled me as moody and sensitive.	I felt unseen, so I reacted by hiding my pain.

My hopes as a child	Did my hope come true? (Yes or No)	What actually happened?	When my hopes were destroyed, I felt and reacted…

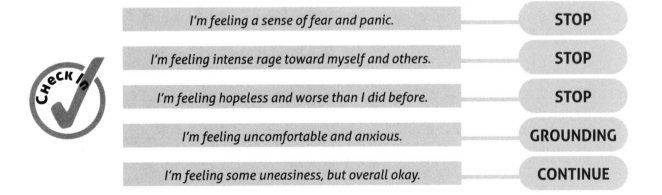

Overcoming Learned Helplessness

You are not alone if you experience revictimization, whether sexual or physical abuse, as an adult after surviving childhood abuse (MacGinley, Breckenridge, and Mowell 2019). If this has happened to you, it's likely that you began to believe that you would always be a victim or that you would always feel powerless in other aspects of your life. Although this is a common reaction, you can transform this thinking!

As a child, you were a victim at the hands of others, which may have created a feeling of powerlessness (Karakurt and Silver 2014; Youinque Foundation 2017). When you were abused, you might have believed that if you did something specific the abuse would stop. Maybe you tried it, and the abuse didn't stop. Over time, you may have felt as if you have no control over what happens to you. You may now believe you cannot change most aspects of your life. This reaction is known as *learned helplessness*. If this feeling has trickled into your adulthood, it's possible that it has created the behavior of "inaction." This inaction can result in missed opportunities for freedom and growth.

Although this "giving up" is a common reaction, you have the power now to choose to believe that you are a *survivor*. By believing that you've transformed from a victim into the survivor you are today, you'll realize that you have the power to choose what you would like for your life.

Hope in Adulthood

Circumstances in your life may have contributed to you feeling the need to set aside hope. Now that you're an adult, it's time to consider being hopeful. As scary as that may seem, consider the possible outcomes that may arise if you allow yourself the opportunity to hope again. If your hopes were destroyed again, would that be any different than what you've already experienced? Could it possibly be better, since you're not in the position of powerlessness anymore?

When you consider the possibility of hoping again, what emotions come to mind?

_____

What do you imagine might be the worst thing that could happen if your hopes were shattered again?

_____

_____

_____

In what ways would a life of hope and fulfillment improve your quality of life?

_____

_____

_____

_____

On a scale of 0 to 10, 0 being not hopeful about the future and 10 being very hopeful about the future, indicate your level of hope today:

_____.

I'm feeling a sense of fear and panic.	**STOP**
I'm feeling intense rage toward myself and others.	**STOP**
I'm feeling hopeless and worse than I did before.	**STOP**
I'm feeling uncomfortable and anxious.	**GROUNDING**
I'm feeling some uneasiness, but overall okay.	**CONTINUE**

Check In

Establishing Hope for the Future

Before you consider the hopes you might have for the future, let's look at the different types of hope. Some hopes are realistic and attainable. Other hopes are unrealistic; these are typically things we wish could happen but are unlikely to occur. For instance, hoping that you can have a healthy intimate relationship is realistic, but hoping that you will inherit billions of dollars and never have to work again is idealistic.

Think about the present moment in your life. Take time now to applaud yourself for the growth you've made to get to this point in your life. Close your eyes and imagine what it would be like to feel hopeful once more. When you open your eyes, give yourself permission to hope. Then write down a list of all realistic hopes that come to mind.

_____

_____

_____

_____

_____

_____

_____

_____

_____

Review your hopes. How does it feel to see them written out? Do any seem more idealistic than realistic? Do any seem within your reach, perhaps more so than when you started this workbook? Did any realistic hopes arise that you had abandoned and that you now feel more prepared to work toward?

Being Hopeful and Reaching Your Goals

Goals do not materialize by simply wishing they would happen. To accomplish a goal, you need to feel hopeful that any action you take is a step closer toward achieving your goal. Hope is a motivator. When you feel motivated and hopeful, you'll be more willing to make the necessary changes needed to ensure your goals can come to pass. It starts by simply believing that healing is possible.

Goal setting is one way you can practice taking steps toward making your hope for the future happen. For example, let's say I hope that if I become a clinical psychologist, I would be able to help other survivors heal. My *hope* is to help other survivors heal. My *goal* is to become a clinical psychologist. Assuming I had not been to college before, the *small steps* I would need to take are:

1. Enroll at a community college or university.

2. Attend and participate in classes.

3. Complete required psychology coursework.

This goal takes years to achieve. However, if I focus on my hope of making a difference and helping survivors heal, this hope serves as a motivator and guides me in becoming a clinical psychologist.

To prevent yourself from becoming discouraged and overwhelmed, it's best to take small steps toward a goal and start with a short-term ambition versus one that would take months or years to achieve. Often, we want something so badly that we jump in, and when it doesn't happen in the time frame we would like, we become discouraged and quit. Then we might say, "I knew having hope wouldn't make this happen. I shouldn't have tried." This type of thinking might prevent us from taking the next steps needed to reach the goal, when the truth is that we jumped in without taking the time to go slow and steady.

In my case, I would revisit my goal to something more attainable in the short term. For example, I could support survivors by volunteering for the National Sexual Assault Hotline (RAINN). Through RAINN, I could train to provide anonymous crisis support to survivors across the country. While my long-term goal may be to become a clinical psychologist, volunteering is an attainable short-term goal that allows me to fulfill my hope of helping survivors.

It is possible to achieve your goals if you have hope. The reason for this is that once you've achieved a goal, you may feel that anything is possible, including healing the wounds caused by sexual abuse. Before you begin the next exercise, make sure your goal is attainable and can be done in a short amount of time. It can help to consider these questions:

1. Which goal would I most likely be able to achieve in a short amount of time?

2. Are there obstacles that might get in the way of achieving this goal? If so, what can I do to still work toward it while considering these obstacles?

3. To ensure that the goal I hope to achieve will be achieved, what small steps can I take?

Write down two short-term goals. You can use the example I gave and the hopes you identified in Establishing Hope for the Future.

The first short-term goal that I *hope* to work toward is: _____

_____

_____

In order to achieve this goal, here are the *small steps* I need to take:

1. _____

2. _____

3. _____

4. _____

The second short-term goal that I *hope* to work toward is: _____

_____

_____

In order to achieve this goal, here are the *small steps* I need to take:

1. _____
2. _____
3. _____
4. _____

After considering which short-term goals you can achieve, how you might handle any obstacles that may arise, and how to feel confident during your efforts to achieve these goals, it is now possible for you to turn hope into action. Using the examples as a guide, write a statement of commitment for achieving your goal.

My commitment to a short-term hope or goal: _____

_____

_____

Example: I'm committed to practicing a daily self-care regimen including meditation and daily walks.

The steps I'll take to make this happen, in order, will be:

1. _____
2. _____
3. _____
4. _____

Example:

1. Find a guided meditation on YouTube that feels doable.

2. Set a timer for 12 p.m. to remind me to use the guided meditation.

3. Walk every day before dinnertime.

I'll start working toward my goal on _____ (date).

I hope to accomplish this goal by _____ (date).

I'll know I've achieved my goal when: _____

_____

_____

Example: I'm consistently meditating and walking daily, and I remember before the alarm goes off.

If something comes up and I need to stop working toward this goal for a moment, I might feel

_____ (emotion, such as disappointment), but with hope I can make this goal happen.

Here are the things that are motivating me to achieve this goal:_____

_____

_____

_____

Example: Self-care has helped me cope better with stress in the past, and I'm seeking to reduce my anxiety.

The people and resources I can rely on as a source of support in pursuing my goal:_____

_____

_____

Example: My partner and my friend Alex.

Time to Celebrate

Even if you take more than a few weeks to accomplish your goal, you will feel more hopeful about your future if you give yourself the opportunity to celebrate your efforts. Please work through this section *after* completing a short-term goal. Repeat it for any other goal you reach.

I completed my goal of _____

on _____ (date). I remained hopeful about _____% of the time. As my hope

increased, I noticed that I felt _____ and I thought

_____. I feel _____ (more, less) hopeful that I can achieve my next goal.

On a scale of 0 to 10, 0 being not hopeful about the future and 10 being very hopeful about the future, today I would rate my level of hope as a _____.

I'm feeling a sense of fear and panic.	**STOP**
I'm feeling intense rage toward myself and others.	**STOP**
I'm feeling hopeless and worse than I did before.	**STOP**
I'm feeling uncomfortable and anxious.	**GROUNDING**
I'm feeling some uneasiness, but overall okay.	**CONTINUE**

What Do You Value in Life?

Previously, we discussed how listening to your trauma voice can urge you to respond with a coping strategy that may worsen your long-term suffering. You might be so accustomed to handling intense emotions in this way that you don't believe there is another way. But imagine the response you might have if you had hope that you could choose how to respond to these painful experiences.

Considering your *values* can assist you in making meaningful choices consistent with the direction in which you wish to take your life. Values are not the same as goals because we do not accomplish a value.

Values are a way of being or doing. For example, I value love, and I demonstrate this value by being loving. Being loving toward my friends because I value love is not the same as intentionally deciding to socialize with friends once a week because I want more social interactions. Getting together with friends is an example of a goal because it can be accomplished; being loving is an example of one of my values. Knowing what is important to you can motivate you to make difficult but necessary changes that can lead to positive well-being (McKay and West 2016).

Using the values chart, circle five to ten of your core values.

Values Chart

Achievement	Adventure	Assertiveness
Acceptance	Belonging	Calmness
Compassion	Commitment	Connection
Control	Cooperation	Creativity
Dependability	Determination	Diversity
Efficiency	Empathy	Excitement
Fairness	Forgiveness	Freedom
Gratitude	Growth	Happiness
Hard work	Health	Honesty
Humility	Independence	Intelligence
Intimacy	Intuition	Justice
Kindness	Love	Loyalty
Mindfulness	Obedience	Persistence
Professionalism	Respect	Restraint
Safety	Security	Self-awareness
Self-control	Sensitivity	Stability
Teamwork	Thoughtfulness	Trust

After identifying your most important values, take a moment to examine the ones you circled. Think about what makes these values so important to you. Do these values reflect happy or difficult times in your life? If so, how?

_____

_____

_____

_____

Describe a time when you acted on these values and received a positive result.

_____

_____

_____

_____

What are some instances when you've neglected to act upon these values? What was the result?

_____

_____

_____

_____

Have you avoided or abandoned these values due to your emotions or desire to avoid?

_____

_____

_____

_____

If so, how often do you feel your life is dictated by emotions rather than values?

_____

_____

_____

_____

I'm feeling a sense of fear and panic.	STOP
I'm feeling intense rage toward myself and others.	STOP
I'm feeling hopeless and worse than I did before.	STOP
I'm feeling uncomfortable and anxious.	GROUNDING
I'm feeling some uneasiness, but overall okay.	CONTINUE

Aligning Your Actions with Your Values

As you learned in previous chapters, automatic trauma responses may influence how you respond to painful emotions and experiences. If you had a choice and could respond to these painful feelings differently, what would you do? How might your life be different if this were the case? Let's explore the answers to these questions now.

To make a different choice, it's important to practice *values-consistent action*: acting on what matters to you rather than acting on emotions (McKay and West 2016). It is possible to accomplish this by being aware of your urge to act and simply observing it without reacting to or judging it. For example, if you value health and have noticed that your way of coping with sadness has been to drink, you can practice values-consistent action by 1) noticing this urge and 2) not acting on it and then 3) refocusing on what matters most to you—in this case, your health. Maybe you have a healthy snack or go for a walk instead. This process is not as easy as it sounds, and it requires a great deal of practice. However, you can cope with painful emotions in an alternative way when you consider what you value before acting (McKay and West 2016).

The values we hold dear influence all aspects of our lives, including relationships, social connections, our work, learning, and our self-care. During the next exercise, you'll identify the areas of your life in which your most important values are reflected and gain an understanding of how your values are reflected in your behavior. Additionally, you'll identify positive outcomes as a result of living according to your values in your most important areas of life. It's ultimately up to you to decide whether and when to align your actions with your values.

As you complete the exercise, practice self-compassion, as there may be a disconnect between your intentions and your actual actions. Consider the reflection questions first. Then, use your answers to determine which values-consistent actions you might take.

Reflect

On a scale of 0 (unimportant) to 5 (very important), with 3 being moderately important, which of the values you circled are very important to you? List them here.

Value	Rating of importance
Example: Connection	4

In which areas of your life do these values hold the most importance? Consider intimate relationships, parenting, friendships, work, family of origin, spirituality or religion, learning, and health or self-care.

Value	Areas of Life
Example: Connection	Intimate relationships, parenting, friendships, work

Now, take a moment to think about how you can put your values into action. What can you do? In the following chart, list your values, the areas of life that are most important to you, and how you can align your actions with them.

Value	Areas of life	Actions I might take
Connection	Intimate relationships	Talk to my partner about my feelings while remaining vulnerable and open.
	Friendships	Arrange time to meet with friends regularly.
	Parenting	Talk to kids with gentleness and love even when I feel disconnected.
	Work	Ask for assistance when I become overwhelmed by tasks.

Value	Areas of life	Actions I might take

Consider how many actions you've taken over the past week that align with these values. On a scale of 0 (no action) to 5 (five or more actions aligned with this value), with 3 equating three actions, which of the values you circled had the most values-consistent actions? Which value has the least action? List them here with their action ratings next to the value.

Value	Rating of Values-Consistent Actions
Example: Connection	2

Obstacles That Get in the Way

Often, we intend to act in a certain way, yet barriers may prevent us from fulfilling that intention. An obstacle may be a result of emotions, perceptions, or practical factors, such as a lack of time. In order to live according to your values, you need to reflect on what often prevents you from doing so.

Using the previous exercise as a guide, select your most meaningful values, then commit to the values-consistent actions you selected. Use the chart that follows to determine the actions you will commit to that align with your most important values. Make a list of any potential obstacles you may encounter. Write down any steps you can take to overcome or accept these obstacles while still pursuing your values.

Dealing with Obstacles

Commitment	Potential Obstacles	Steps to Overcome or Accept Obstacles
To align with my values of openness and connection, I commit to being more vulnerable by talking to my partner about my feelings.	When I share my thoughts and feelings, I'm concerned that my partner will criticize or leave me.	If I am criticized, I'm willing to accept it may be painful, but enduring pain to stand up for what I believe in may be worth it if I value openness. I can use self-soothing techniques to help me cope.

I'm feeling a sense of fear and panic.	**STOP**
I'm feeling intense rage toward myself and others.	**STOP**
I'm feeling hopeless and worse than I did before.	**STOP**
I'm feeling uncomfortable and anxious.	**GROUNDING**
I'm feeling some uneasiness, but overall okay.	**CONTINUE**

Check In

Keeping a Hope Journal

Even if you feel that you have little to look forward to or that fear often prevents you from hoping for a better future, you can still work toward hope. Fear is a valid feeling given your past experiences. The first thing you can do for yourself is to honor that fear. It's there for a reason and deserves to be acknowledged. However, that fear may be hindering your growth as an adult. Consider the ways hope could help bring about greater well-being in your life today. Think about whether that fear continues to be helpful or unhelpful. A hope journal is a great way to discover the answers you may need to set aside any residual fear, so that you can cultivate hope in your life.

For two to three weeks, use the prompts below to begin a *daily* hope journal. After this time, if you no longer need the prompts, please keep writing; doing so will continue to build hope and motivation, and lessen fears and doubts.

Write about the challenges you've faced. Describe your three highest hopes and three deepest fears related to the challenges.

_____

_____

_____

_____

_____

_____

_____

_____

Describe how your family culture or upbringing may have influenced your ability to disclose abuse and hope for change.

_____

_____

_____

_____

_____

_____

_____

_____

What gives you hope? What could potentially motivate you to hope?

_____

_____

_____

_____

_____

_____

_____

_____

What are the benefits of hoping?

_____

_____

_____

_____

_____

_____

_____

_____

_____

Recall a time when you felt hopeful. Describe your thoughts, feelings, and actions related to that moment. Include the outcome and how you handled it.

_____

_____

_____

_____

_____

_____

_____

What are the risks of having hope? How can you accept them while remaining hopeful?

_____

_____

_____

_____

_____

_____

_____

_____

_____

Tying It All Together

Throughout this workbook, you've been working on strategies that can rebuild hope into your life. The most important thing to keep in mind as you work toward healing is that you already have the capacity to hope within you. Remember, hope can mean the difference between hanging on and giving up, and you are here, so you didn't give up!

Having hope doesn't mean always being positive or believing the best outcome will always happen. Having hope simply means that you believe you will heal and want something better for your life.

In the next chapter, you'll learn mindfulness skills for practicing being fully present, strengthening your prefrontal cortex, and transforming inactive thinking into active thinking. By liberating your mind from thoughts and emotions that keep you feeling powerless, you can reduce distress and trauma responses when faced with stressful situations.

Before we move on, let's assess your feelings and goals related to the emergence of hope in your life. Answer the following questions:

What feelings did I have as I thought about shattered hopes from the past? Do I feel the same now as I did then? If not, how do I feel differently now and why?

_____

_____

_____

_____

_____

What did I learn about the benefits of hope? How can having hope improve my life?

_____

_____

_____

_____

_____

What did I learn about converting my hopes into goals? What commitments have I made to set a goal? What steps have I already taken to work toward a goal?

_____

_____

_____

_____

What feelings did I have when I listed my realistic hopes? What was hard about this for me? What have I done that I'm proud of and want to continually celebrate?

_____

_____

_____

_____

What values do I hold? Are my actions currently aligned with these values? If not, what can I do to ensure I am living according to what is important to me?

_____

_____

_____

_____

What do I need to do to take care of myself and ensure that I'm practicing self-care (for example, spend time outdoors, meditate, take a break from this workbook)?

_____

_____

_____

_____

_____

| On a scale of 1 to 10, rate your level of hope both *before* you began this chapter and *currently*.

    1 = feeling completely hopeless

    10 = feeling extremely hopeful | Before the chapter _____

After the chapter _____ |

CHAPTER 6

Mindfulness

"You can't stop the waves, but you can learn how to surf."

—Jon Kabat-Zinn

The practice of *mindfulness* can teach you how to stay grounded in the present versus focusing on the past. Mindfulness is the ability to be fully present, aware of where you are and what you are doing, and not be reactive to the things going on around you.

During childhood, your survival depended on you developing coping skills to deal with the abuse and messages you were receiving, which might have presented as unwanted thoughts and feelings. However, these same coping strategies that helped you survive a childhood of powerlessness may not be helpful in adulthood.

Mindfulness is about turning inward, facing your fear, and learning how to relate differently to unwanted thoughts and feelings. During the practice of mindfulness, you can focus on inspiring thoughts and feelings while consciously choosing to be okay with any unhelpful thoughts and feelings that might arise. Regardless of what has happened to you or might be occurring in your environment now, you can choose how to respond. This statement is not meant to minimize your experience in any way. It is merely meant to inspire and help you take back the control that you lacked as a child. In this chapter, you'll learn how mindfulness can improve your resilience to stress and help you manage triggers.

Transforming Your Brain

In chapter 3, you learned that trauma affects how the brain develops, functions, and reacts to our perceptions and thoughts. In fact, triggering thoughts and feelings can activate the limbic system, the part of the brain involved in emotional and behavioral responses. Our thoughts trigger reactions in our brain, which are carried through our body and can result in emotions and behaviors. In other words, when you pay attention to a particular thought, the brain changes and learns how to respond to that thought in a healthy or unhealthy manner. The brain does not interpret if a thought is healthy or unhealthy, it simply reacts.

Mindfulness will help strengthen the prefrontal cortex and teach it to be aware of and manage the reactive limbic system, which will reduce the occurrence and length of those triggers (Tang 2017; Younique Foundation 2017). Mindfulness helps the brain change! Mindfulness teaches you how to concentrate and regulate your thoughts. It can be challenging to learn how to focus on some thoughts while letting others go, but it can happen with practice. Part of your healing process means learning how to be aware of and manage thoughts. Being mindful of your thoughts is another way you can take charge of your life.

The Myths and Truths of Mindfulness

You may have heard falsehoods about mindfulness that have prevented you from giving it a try. Let's look at some popular myths (Bernhard 2014) as well as the facts.

MYTHS

- **Myth #1: Mindfulness is in conflict with certain religions.** Although mindfulness was originally taught by the Buddha, there is no specific belief system associated with it. It is simply a technique that teaches you how to focus on the present moment.

- **Myth #2: Mindfulness is easy.** Remembering to be mindful and committing to a daily practice can be very challenging, but it gets easier with practice. You're developing a new habit and transforming how your brain operates, which takes time. Mindfulness is like weight training—eventually the muscles will form. You're exercising your brain and building how it functions.

- **Myth #3: During meditation is the only time mindfulness is practiced.** Not so. Practicing mindfulness can happen while doing everyday tasks, such as eating, walking, working, and doing any activity you enjoy. By practicing mindfulness in everything you do, you increase your awareness of the things your mind may be thinking while doing those activities, and your mind begins to quiet down. Imagine what it would be like to walk on the beach and hear the waves crashing without disruptive thoughts bringing you down. Being mindful does not mean eradicating thoughts but recognizing bodily and sensory sensations as well as thoughts as they arise.

- **Myth #4: All psychological issues can be treated with mindfulness.** Indeed, mindfulness is a useful way for you to become aware of things you may be thinking and believing, so that you don't react to every thought or emotion that arises. However, when your mind becomes quiet, it might bring up feelings and thoughts related to your sexual abuse that you were not aware of. This may cause distress and anxiety. It's important to understand that your mind has kept busy with negative thoughts and emotions as a way of protecting you. If this happens and you feel intense feelings of anxiousness or fear, respond to yourself with kindness, acknowledge what you've been through, and talk to a support system person or a mental health professional.

TRUTHS

- **Truth #1: Mindfulness is evidence-based and could have health benefits.** Many researchers have studied the benefits of mindfulness, and results have consistently shown that mindfulness may contribute to greater physical and mental health, improved brain function, increased immunity, and reductions in stress and emotional reactivity (Tang 2017).

- **Truth #2: Being mindful is not a unique characteristic that only some people possess.** You already have the capacity to be present. In fact, we all do. You don't have to change who you are to practice mindfulness. By practicing mindfulness, you may discover an innate ability you were unaware you possessed.

- **Truth #3: Mindfulness nurtures and acknowledges the best of who you are.** You may have experienced increased stress if you've tried to join a group or use a remedy (such as a fad diet) that requires you to change who you are or become something you're not. These types of remedies may fail because you are not true to yourself. Mindfulness is not that! Mindfulness acknowledges who you are right now and supports you through the journey of awareness.

- **Truth #4: Consistent mindfulness seems to increase resiliency to stress.** There is evidence that mindfulness and meditation increase resilience. The more mindfulness and meditation you practice, the more resilient your brain becomes (Tang 2017). The more you practice mindfulness, the easier it will become for you to overcome intense emotions and thoughts and begin to feel grounded.

Reflect

Describe your previous experience with mindfulness:

_____

_____

_____

_____

_____

If you've tried it, what feelings come up as you read about the benefits?

_____

_____

_____

_____

Building Hope and Resilience with Mindfulness Practice

Mindfulness does not necessarily prevent you from feeling physical or psychological reactions to difficulties, but it can help the body and mind spring back from distressing situations (Oh, Sarwar, and Pervez 2022). You've already learned that mindfulness can rewire how the brain operates, but you're probably wondering how it can reduce stress. Chapter 3 demonstrated how abuse can trigger the automatic response of fight, flight, freeze, or fawn, and how the amygdala processes strong emotions and activates this response by releasing stress hormones. A mindfulness practice diminishes activity in the amygdala and increases the connections between the amygdala and prefrontal cortex. In other words, mindfulness helps you to be less reactive to stressors and recover better from stress when you experience it.

As a means of understanding the relationship between mindfulness, hope, and resilience, it might be helpful to take a closer look at what each of these terms mean.

- **Mindfulness:** maintaining a moment-by-moment awareness of your thoughts, feelings, bodily sensations, and surrounding environment through a compassionate lens.

- **Resilience:** bouncing back from adverse life events or recovering quickly from difficulties.

- **Hope:** the belief that your future will be better than the present and that you have the ability to make it happen.

Stress and traumatic memories can lead to negative stories about yourself and others. These stories can lead to replaying the conversation throughout the day in your mind, perpetuating anxiety and low mood far more than necessary. When practiced regularly, mindfulness reduces this repetitive thinking, making you more resilient to future stressful events. By slowing down your brain, mindfulness allows you to bounce back from daily stressors and gives you more space to make the changes you want so you can achieve your goals. Mindfulness and hope make you more resilient so that, in the future when difficulties arise, you'll be able to cope with them.

Everyday Mindfulness Practices

While there are many different types of mindfulness practices, starting with a basic one will help you gain confidence and increase your ability to remain in the present moment. The exercises provided will give you an opportunity to explore options for a daily mindfulness practice. In fact, if you've been doing the exercises in this workbook, you'll have already come across two mindfulness practices: Mindful Acceptance Meditation (chapter 2) and Self-Soothing Toolbox (chapter 3). In this chapter you'll learn seven more basic mindfulness techniques:

- 5-4-3-2-1 Technique

- Body Scan

- Deep Breathing

- Alternate-Nostril Beathing

- Mindful Journaling

- Two-Minute Meditation

- Compassion-Focused Meditation

Please try each one! Each person can react differently to these practices. For some survivors, a practice may not work at all. Give each a few tries to discover which one is most helpful to you.

5-4-3-2-1 Technique

This exercise is also known as Five Senses. It is a quick and easy mindfulness practice that can be done nearly anywhere. With the 5-4-3-2-1 Technique, you'll intentionally take in the details of your environment with each of your five senses. You'll pay attention to features that your mind would normally ignore, such as faint sounds or the texture of a common object, instead of thoughts or emotions that may be inducing your stress.

Practice this exercise at least once per day for a week. The more often you practice, the more you'll become aware of things around you. Try to observe in the order provided, but if you find that one sense is easier to explore than another, work with that sense until you feel more confident attempting the others. In moments of stress, this is a simple activity that can help you feel more grounded.

Sight	**What are 5 things you can see?** Bring your attention to five things that you can see around you. Pick something that you don't normally notice, like a pattern on the ceiling or a small crack in the sidewalk.
Touch	**What are 4 things you can physically feel?** Bring awareness to four things that your body senses, like the sensation of the clothing on your body, the breeze on your skin, or the chair you're sitting in.
Hear	**What are 3 things you can hear?** Take a moment to listen and note three things that you hear in the background. Listen for sounds your mind typically tunes out, such as the chirp of a bird, trees blowing in the wind, or distant traffic from a nearby road.
Smell	**What are 2 things you can smell?** Bring your awareness to smells that you usually filter out, whether they're pleasant or unpleasant. Notice the smells in the air around you, like freshly mowed grass or an air freshener. If nothing is apparent, you can seek out something with a scent, such as a candle or flower.
Taste	**What is 1 thing you can taste?** Carry gum, candy, or small snacks for this step. Pop one in your mouth and focus closely on the flavors.

After a week of practice, complete the following questions about your mindful experience using your senses with awareness and intention:

One thing I was able to *see* that I had not noticed before was: _____

_____

_____

One thing I was able to *feel* that I had not been aware of before was: _____

_____

_____

One thing I was able to *hear* that I had tuned out before was: _____

_____

_____

One thing that I was able to *smell* that I had not noticed before was: _____

_____

_____

One thing that I was able to *taste* that I had not paid attention to before was: _____

_____

_____

Body Scan

This practice, adapted from one of Jon Kabat-Zinn's approaches to mindfulness, will teach you how to set time aside for yourself and practice the nurturing that you deserve. Try to let go of judgment and critical thoughts as best as you can. Just be aware of what you're experiencing. There is no right way to feel while doing this. Give yourself permission to be and feel whatever you feel. If you feel tension in a place you haven't noticed before, accept it and let it be without judgment.

Make sure you're in a quiet spot where you will not be disrupted. If you become drowsy during the exercise, open your eyes so that you can remain awake and aware. The first time you do this, you may need to read step by step, but as you remember the steps, you'll be able to do this with your eyes closed and experience the scan on a deeper level. If you have difficulty following the steps, you may record yourself reading it and then play the recording while practicing, or you can access a free audio track of this meditation at http://www.newharbinger.com/53790.

1. Lying on your back, place your palms facing up and your feet slightly apart. If you prefer to be seated, sit in a chair with your feet resting on the floor. Be as still as possible through the exercise. If you need to adjust your position, do so with awareness of what you are moving and why.

2. Bring your awareness to your breath as you breathe in and out naturally. There is no need to change your breathing. Just become aware of the breath itself. Notice the rise and fall of your abdomen as you breathe. As you lie or sit there, see if you can bring your awareness to your body as a whole. Be with your body just as it is, moment by moment and breath by breath.

3. Notice how your body feels resting against the surface of where you're lying or sitting. Notice how your body presses against the surface. Notice the texture of your clothing against your

skin. Notice the temperature in the room and how it feels on your body. Notice any thoughts that arise, then bring your attention back to the breath.

4. Now, shift your attention to your toes. Notice any sensation you feel, such as the toes touching each other, warmth, coldness, tingling, or numbness. Whatever it is you feel, notice the sensation. It's okay if you don't feel anything at all, just notice the lack of sensation. When you feel something, take note of whether it is pleasant or unpleasant. Be aware of any emotional reactions that arise, such as boredom, impatience, judging yourself, or sadness. Allow these feelings to be held in awareness without judgment as you stay in the present moment.

5. When you're ready to move on, notice your breath. On the exhale, shift your focus to the top of your feet and ankles. Notice any sensations or lack of sensations, just like you did with your toes. Remember to bring your attention back to the region of focus any time your thoughts take you elsewhere.

6. When you're ready, take a natural breath in. On the exhale, let go of this region of the body as you shift your focus to your lower legs. Notice the presence of your calf and skin. Be open to whatever sensations are there and accept whatever you feel moment by moment.

7. Again, when you're ready, on an out-breath, let go of this region and shift your focus to your knees and thighs. Open to any sensations in the knees and thighs as you breathe. Feel the kneecaps and the sides of the knees. Notice your upper thighs as they press against the surface on which you're lying or sitting.

8. When you're ready, on an out-breath, let go of this region and shift your focus to your pelvic region. Be aware of the hips, the buttocks, the tailbone, the pelvic bone, and the genitals. Bring your awareness to whatever sensations you may feel in these areas.

9. When you're ready, exhale and let go of this region as you shift your focus to your lower back. This region can hold a lot of tension. See if you notice any and, if so, let it be as you become aware of the sensations you feel. As you breathe out, let go of the back.

10. Move your focus to your chest and abdomen. Notice any sensation you may experience, such as a particular heaviness or lightness. Sink into the stillness and awareness, and let yourself just be.

11. Now, move your attention to the heart, lungs, muscles, and bloodstream. Just see if you can notice the beat of your heart and the way your lungs move as you breathe. Notice any emotions that arise as you stay with this area.

12. Take in a long breath, hold it for a second, and then release. Bring your attention to your hands. Feel the sensations of the fingers, palms, back of hands, and wrists. Notice any

sensations before moving attention to the arms, including the lower and upper arms and elbows. See if you can notice the entire arm from the fingertips to the shoulders. Bring awareness to any sensations that may exist there.

13. When you're ready, on an out-breath, shift your focus to your neck. Linger here for a moment and acknowledge any feeling that may exist before turning your focus to your face and head. This is another region that stores tension in the course of a day. Notice the slackness or tightness of the jaw. Bring awareness to the mouth, nose, cheeks, ears, eyes, forehead, scalp, and back and top of the head. Allow this region to be as it is and notice any sensations and feelings you may feel. When you're ready, let it go and just sit with awareness itself.

14. Hold awareness for the body as a whole, from the toes to the top of your head. Embrace your body as it is and how it feels in this moment. Just rest in awareness and stillness. Feel the openness to just be in the stillness. As you remain still, take a moment to praise yourself for taking this time to nurture yourself. Acknowledge this effort you've made and notice if you feel the desire to continue this practice regularly. Rest here as long as you choose in stillness and silence.

15. When you're ready to come back to the room, open your eyes and sit up.

This exercise is not meant to be assessed or evaluated. It's meant for you to notice and allow your body and mind to be just as it is. If you would like, reflect on what you felt, or notice if you were able to just let the experience be what it was without questioning it. You can also bring to your awareness any areas in your body that offered surprising or upsetting sensations, such as pain, tension, or throbbing. Next time you do this exercise, see if you notice the same sensations in the same areas.

Breathing Techniques

An effective way to reduce stress comes from something we do naturally without much thought: breathing. When done as a mentally active process, breathing techniques can leave the body feeling calm, focused, and relaxed. This state of calmness occurs through deep breathing by providing an increased supply of oxygen to your brain, which stimulates the parasympathetic nervous system into a calm state. In addition, it can bring your awareness away from your thoughts and feelings, thereby quieting your mind.

You can practice deep breathing any time and anywhere you're feeling anxious or stressed. It can be very beneficial for those who have experienced traumatic events, as it can help you cope with thoughts or emotions that may arise. Even though you can use these techniques any time you need, it's recommended that you practice at least one of the following techniques once daily until you discover the technique that works best for you.

Deep Breathing

When we get scared, our body begins to panic and we breathe shallowly, which can cause dizziness. Practicing breathing slowly and deeply will help you reduce panic and stress. You can do this breathing exercise with your eyes closed or open. Choose whichever makes you feel most comfortable and grounded in this moment. Here's how to do it:

1. Sit in a comfortable position or lie down.

2. Place your right hand on your stomach and your left hand on your chest. Imagine you have a balloon in your stomach, inflating as you breathe in and deflating as you breathe out.

3. Breathe in slowly through your nose. Notice your stomach expand as you inhale. (Note: if you're breathing from your stomach, the hand on your stomach will move, but the hand on your chest will not.)

4. Focus your attention on filling your lungs with air.

5. Slowly exhale, releasing all the air through your mouth.

6. Practice breathing one full inhale for five to seven seconds and exhale for five to seven seconds.

7. Repeat steps 3 to 7 up to ten times.

Note: If you become lightheaded, return to normal breathing before attempting to resume this practice.

Alternate-Nostril Breathing

This is another breathing technique for relaxation. This strategy might be useful in moments of stress or anxiety, especially if you're experiencing an increased heart rate. Alternate-nostril breathing has been shown to improve cardiovascular function and reduce heart rate. If you're feeling sick or congested, you should refrain from this exercise until the congestion has cleared. Follow these steps:

1. Start in a seated position.

2. Using your right hand, extend your thumb and ring finger toward your nose, with remaining fingers curled into a fist.

3. Breathe in.

4. Upon exhale, press your right thumb gently against your right nostril, blocking airflow.

5. Then, inhale through your left nostril.

6. Next, close your left nostril with your right ring finger while releasing your thumb, then exhale through your right nostril.

7. Inhale through your right nostril. You've completed one cycle.

8. Repeat steps 4 through 7.

9. Continue this breathing pattern for up to five minutes or until calm.

Mindful Journaling

Journaling is one of the easiest ways to start and maintain a regular practice of mindfulness. It can help you turn your attention inward, increase positive thoughts, decrease negative thoughts, and improve concentration. Some people prefer to write and others prefer to draw. Either is beneficial.

Mindful journaling is a way to create a space to have an open and straightforward dialogue with yourself. It can help you to become more aware of triggering thoughts and feelings, and express yourself without worry of judgment and expectation. By journaling, you can provide yourself the acceptance and self-compassion you deserve. It can be difficult to start this process if you don't already have a journaling practice. A good first step is to set a schedule for journaling, for example, every day at lunchtime or every morning while drinking coffee or tea. Here are more tips to get you started:

1. Begin by putting yourself in a mindful space. Ground yourself by focusing on your breath. Take a deep breath, and on the exhale release any judgments or expectations for yourself.

2. Focus on being present. Try not to think about anything you may have to do that day.

3. Allow your mind to gravitate toward whatever it is you feel you need to express.

4. As you begin writing, notice if there are any thoughts trying to pull your attention away from the task. Are you feeling uncomfortable or anxious? If so, honor this feeling and write about those emotions.

5. If emotions or topics aren't coming naturally, or you want direction, consider the following journaling prompts:

    • Focus on something around you, such as a pet or a tree outside your window. Describe it.

    • Describe three urges that you noticed and did not judge or act on today.

    • Describe three actions by others that made you feel loved today.

- Describe three things that were challenging today.

- I'm proud of myself for…

- If my body had a voice, it would say…

- I forgive myself for…

- My greatest strengths are…

- I could be kinder to myself by…

- I'm no longer afraid to…

- I know I'm capable of…

- I nurture myself by…

- I'm committed to trying to…

- I listen to my intuition by…

- I feel joy and happiness when…

- I'm aware that…

- I'm practicing self-care by…

- I'm hopeful that…

- I believe that I can…

Use the Mindful Journaling Log to help you keep track of your commitment to daily journaling, how long you spend writing, and what to do if you get stuck. You may download a free copy of this log at http://www.newharbinger.com/53790.

Mindful Journaling Log

Date	Time of day I journaled at…	Minutes I wrote for…	Reflection When I got stuck, I…	Commitment I'll stick with it for…
March 8	9:45 p.m.	15 minutes	doodled	1 week

Date	Time of day	Minutes	Reflection	Commitment
	I journaled at…	I wrote for…	When I got stuck, I…	I'll stick with it for…

After a week of journaling, complete the following statements to assess your ability to use journaling as a mindfulness strategy:

When I journaled this week, I was able to turn inward about _____% of the time. I discovered

that _____ helped me stay in the present moment and

_____ often led me to be distracted.

While journaling I noticed I had positive thoughts about:

_____

_____

_____

_____

While journaling I noticed I had unhelpful thoughts about:

_____

_____

_____

_____

Begin a Meditation Practice

The practice of meditation helps you increase awareness so that you can focus on cultivating your mind rather than nurturing thoughts and feelings that prevent you from feeling hopeful. You can practice this in two ways: 1) focusing your attention on your breath, and each time your mind wanders, you bring your attention back to your breath, or 2) training your mind to be okay with wherever it goes without focusing on anything.

Meditation can help you see yourself more clearly by learning how to quiet the noise (constant thoughts) and witness your thoughts without judgment. By doing this, you'll start to understand your deepest desires, needs, and areas for improvement. Increasing self-awareness can help you make helpful choices that could impact how you feel about yourself and others.

Now that you've practiced what being mindful means and some techniques that help increase your ability to be mindful, you're ready to learn how to focus on quieting your mind through meditation. How often you decide to meditate is strictly up to you. While some people choose to meditate daily, others meditate once a week. The choice is yours, but the more you practice meditation, the easier it becomes.

It is important to honor your body. A calm mind and being aware of the present moment can be overwhelming and terrifying for survivors, especially if it activates trauma thoughts during meditation. If you notice this occurring as you start this practice, yoga may be a better alternative. Since yoga focuses on movement and breathing, it may assist you in coping with physiological sensations that may be present in your body (van der Kolk 2014). When you learn how to tolerate these sensations, the sensations cease to be a trigger, and that part of the body becomes safe and less traumatized. With the next few activities, you'll be able to begin your meditation practice by bringing your attention to your breath.

Two-Minute Meditation

Read the instructions all the way through first, then begin practicing by setting a two-minute timer.

1. Get in a comfortable position. You can sit in a chair or on the floor. Close your eyes or keep them open if you feel more comfortable being able to focus on something in the room.

2. Focus on your breath. Notice where you feel your breath most. Is it in your belly or your chest? Try to keep your attention on your inhale and exhale.

3. Follow your breath for two minutes. Start by taking in a deep inhale, expanding your stomach, and then exhaling slowly. After two deep controlled breaths, breathe in your natural rhythm for the remainder of the time.

4. When the timer goes off, open your eyes, and reflect on your experience by answering the following questions.

Reflect

How long was it before your mind drifted away from your breath?

_____

What thoughts or feelings arose before you were able to bring your attention back to your breath?

_____

_____

_____

_____

Were you successful at bringing your attention to your breath and away from your thoughts? If you were, how do you think focusing on the breath helped you quiet your mind?

_____

_____

If you were not able to focus back on your breath, what do you think would help you do that? Shorter meditation time? Grounding or journaling your thoughts before beginning your practice?

_____

_____

Practice the Two-Minute Meditation for several days to a week. Once you feel confident that you can direct your focus to your breath, move to the next meditation practice.

Compassion-Focused Meditation

Compassion-focused meditation is one way to become aware of feelings and thoughts that may weigh you down and learn how to cultivate compassion toward yourself. Begin with a five-minute practice session. When you begin to notice your thoughts without judging them, and you're able to provide yourself with the kindness you deserve, increase the time in five-minute intervals with each successful session.

1. Take a seat. Pick a spot that is comfortable and has minimal distractions. Close your eyes or keep them open if you prefer.

2. Set a time limit. Start with five or ten minutes and increase the time in five-minute increments each time you feel like doing so.

3. Bring awareness to your body. Whether you're sitting in a chair with your feet touching the ground, sitting on the floor cross-legged, or kneeling, notice any sensations that you might be feeling in your body. Note them without judgment.

4. Bring awareness to your breath. Breathe in deeply. Notice the movement of your stomach. As you exhale slowly, notice any sensations you may feel. Follow the rhythm of your breath as you breathe in and out.

5. Notice if your mind wanders. This is normal. One minute you may be focused on your breath, and the next you're thinking, "I still have to do laundry." When this happens, tell your mind, "I see that thought." Then return your attention back to your breath.

6. Be kind to yourself, even if your mind wanders often. Try not to judge yourself. Even if the thought is negative in nature, gently and kindly let yourself be okay with that thought, and then return your attention to your breath.

7. When the timer goes off, offer yourself kindness. When you're ready, bring your attention back to the space you're in. If your eyes were closed, open them. Look around the room, note any sounds you hear. Notice how your body feels in this moment. Notice any thoughts or feelings you are experiencing. Reflect on your experience by answering the following questions.

Reflect

How long was your first meditation session using this technique? Were you able to increase the time limit? If so to what and when?

_____

_____

How long was it before your mind drifted away from your breath?

_____

What thoughts or feelings arose before you were able to bring your attention back to your breath?

_____

_____

_____

Were you successful at bringing your attention to your breath and away from your thoughts? If you were, how do you think focusing on the breath helped you quiet your mind?

_____

_____

Did you provide yourself with kindness and compassion? If so, how did you do that or what did you tell yourself that was nurturing?

_____

_____

_____

_____

The following Mindfulness Practice Log will help you keep track of your practice. Record what you observed while practicing and how long you were mindful each day. Check the last column if you found this practice to be useful, relaxing, or successful at reducing distress associated with a common trigger. If you wish to continue practicing, which is encouraged, and require more space, you can access this log at http://www.newharbinger.com/53790.

Mindfulness Practice Log

Date	Type of practice	What did you notice in your mind, body, and feelings?	Total minutes practiced	Was it relaxing or stress-reducing? (✓)

Date	Type of practice	What did you notice in your mind, body, and feelings?	Total minutes practiced	Was it relaxing or stress-reducing? (✓)

Tying It All Together

In this chapter, you practiced enhancing your ability to be present, which means understanding where you are and learning how to focus your attention to aspects that can ground you to the present moment. By practicing mindfulness, you're strengthening the prefrontal cortex and learning how to train the brain to regulate your thoughts.

If you've been practicing mindfulness regularly through this workbook, you may be more aware of the chatting that takes place in your mind, and you may have developed a way to manage this noise through mindfulness. Through these practices, you may also be more aware of things you hadn't noticed before because your mind had been keeping you too busy to notice certain things in your environment. Maybe you're now noticing the sounds of birds around you, the way the sun reflects off water, or the way your blanket feels against your skin. All these things surround us every day, but when we are lost in our own thoughts and feelings, we often neglect to notice them.

Mindfulness is a way to bring your awareness to this moment. If you find a practice that works, stick with it. This is an excellent indication that mindfulness practices allow you to heal and focus more on the present than the past.

The following questions will help you assess your feelings and goals related to practicing mindfulness in your life. Ask yourself:

What feelings and thoughts did I have that made it difficult to remain mindful?

_____

_____

_____

_____

Do I feel the same now as I did before I started practicing mindfulness? If not, how do I feel differently now and why?

_____

_____

_____

_____

What did I learn about mindfulness? How can being mindful increase hope in my life?

_____

_____

_____

_____

What did I learn about myself? Which technique helped me be in the present moment the most and feel calm?

_____

_____

_____

_____

What goals have I set? How will these goals help me continue using mindfulness to get in touch with myself and keep me feeling grounded?

_____

_____

_____

_____

On a scale of 1 to 10, rate your level of hope both *before* you began this chapter and *currently.*	
1 = feeling completely hopeless	Before the chapter _____
10 = feeling extremely hopeful	After the chapter _____

Dear Reader

You've completed this workbook! Your newfound awareness of yourself has paved the way for further healing. You may be wondering, "What should I do next?" My suggestion is that you begin by accepting where you are on your journey toward hope and healing. No matter where you are right now, you are closer to where you want to be than you were when you first picked up this workbook. Be proud of the progress you've made, even if you still feel there is more to explore.

This workbook was designed to provide you with support, encouragement, and the tools you need to keep working toward what matters to you. You've prepared yourself for the next chapter of your life through your dedication to practicing coping skills such as self-compassion and mindfulness. You have the tools to nurture, trust, and love yourself whenever you experience painful emotions or thoughts. If you continue to act on what matters to you, you will continue to heal, which will result in greater hope than you may have ever imagined.

Your identity is not defined by what happened to you or the struggles you may still be experiencing. To maintain your focus on hope and healing, ask yourself the following question when you're struggling: *Will I fully accept the things I struggle with, without defense or judgment, and take whatever steps are necessary to move in the direction of my chosen values at this time?*

The journey to where you want to be has begun by you taking this time to honor where you are right now. The hope I have for you is that you continue to do what matters to you and that you realize what I did as a survivor: we are thrivers!

Kind regards,

—Stacey R. Pinatelli, PsyD

Acknowledgments

It is with gratitude that I acknowledge all those who helped me put this workbook together, including family, friends, and mental health professionals. I am particularly grateful to my husband and my children—Serena, Dylan, Alyssa, and Alec—for supporting me despite the limited time we spent together due to years of research and extensive writing.

I am deeply grateful to Hadas Pade, PsyD; Megan Carlos, PhD; and Kevin Bunch, PsyD, for their encouragement, expertise, and feedback, which inspired me to produce something that I believe will benefit many survivors. Further, I would like to acknowledge the generosity of the mental health professionals who generously volunteered to review the original version of this workbook and whose feedback ultimately enabled this workbook to become what I had envisioned it to be: Kate Stanford, LMHC, CCTP, CATP; John Behling, LCSW; Brighton Earley, PhD; Christine M. Fahrenbach, PhD; and Joanna Fava, PhD.

Last, I wish to thank my friends Noelle Schupp, Anna Hopkins, and Lisa Vassiliadis, who have stood by me throughout the years.

Resources

"Sometimes, reaching out and taking someone's hand is the beginning of a journey. At other times, it is allowing another to take yours."

—Vera Nazarian

Survivor's National Hotline

RAINN

(800) 656-HOPE

Our nation's largest anti–sexual violence organization offers confidential support through a free 24-hours-a-day hotline for survivors of sexual abuse, rape, sexual assault, and domestic violence.

Organizations

The following organizations and websites provide resources for survivors of sexual abuse. There is no implicit recommendation or endorsement associated with inclusion on this list.

Road to Recovery, Inc.
https://www.road-to-recovery.org
(862) 368-2800

Road to Recovery offers counseling services to survivors of sexual abuse. It offers a free 24-hours-a-day emergency hotline accessible by phone or text message.

Saprea
https://www.saprea.org

Formerly known as the Younique Foundation, Saprea is a public charity that provides healing services to survivors of childhood sexual abuse through online materials, support groups, and a free four-day in-person retreat.

Adult Survivors of Child Abuse

http://www.ascasupport.org

(415) 928-4576, info@ascasupport.org

Adult Survivors of Child Abuse (ASCA) is a program focused on recovery from childhood abuse, including physical, sexual, or emotional abuse or neglect. The program is accessible regardless of financial situation.

Foundation for Survivors of Abuse (FSA)

https://www.survivingabuse.org/resources

FSA offers a "Hope, Healing, & Moving Forward Without Limitations" program, an education program focused on hope and healing.

Websites

Isurvive

http://www.isurvive.org

Isurvive offers an online peer support forum and resources for survivors learning to thrive. Forums cover topics related to recovery and healing from different types of abuse, including physical, sexual, or emotional abuse.

Time to Tell

https://www.timetotell.org

This website was developed by survivor Donna Jensen to offer writing circles for survivors of incest and sexual abuse so that they may tell their stories. Resources on the site include written survivor stories, events and workshops, a blog, and links to books related to sexual abuse.

Recovery and Support for Adult Survivors and Their Families: Book List

http://www.childmolestationprevention.org/reading-resources

This book list provides links to purchase individual books on healing and recovery for adults sexually abused as children.

Joyful Heart Foundation

http://www.joyfulheartfoundation.org

Through a mind-body-spirit approach, the site offers resources and information geared toward increasing knowledge related to healing and awareness. Survivors can sign up for retreats.

References

Bernhard J. 2014. "7 Myths About Mindfulness." *Psychology Today*, June 5. https://www.psychologytoday
.com/us/blog/turning-straw-gold/201406/7-myths-about-mindfulness.

Bowlby, J. 1973. *Attachment and Loss*. New York: Basic Books.

Bratman, G. N., J. P Hamilton, and G. C. Daily. 2012. "The Impacts of Nature Experience on Human
Cognitive Function and Mental Health." *Annals of the New York Academy of Sciences* 1249: 118–136.
https://texanbynature.org/wp-content/uploads/20216/10/Bratman-et-al-2012-Nature-Experience-
Cognitive-Function-and-Mental-Health-NY-ACAD-SCI.pdf.

Brenner, S. 2019. "5 Unmet Needs That May Cause Psychological Issues in Adulthood." Therapy Group
of NYC, October 29. https://nyctherapy.com/therapists-nyc-blog/5-unmet-needs-that-may-cause
-psychological-issues-in-adulthood.

Davis, L. 1990. *The Courage to Heal Workbook: For Women and Men Survivors of Child Sexual Abuse*.
New York: Harper.

de la Torre-Luque, A., C. Díaz-Piedra, and G. Buela-Casal. 2017. "Effects of Preferred Relaxing Music
After Acute Stress Exposure: A Randomized Controlled Trial." *Psychology of Music* 45(6): 795–813.

Draucker, C. B., D. S. Martsolf, C. Roller, G. Knapik, R. Ross, and A. Warner-Stidham. 2011. "Healing
from Childhood Sexual Abuse: A Theoretical Model." *Journal of Child Sexual Abuse* 20(4): 435–466.

Dreisoerner, A., N. M. Junker, W. Scholtz, J. Heimrich, S. Bloemeke, B. Ditzen, and R. van Dick. 2021.
"Self-Soothing Touch and Being Hugged Reduce Cortisol Responses to Stress: A Randomized
Controlled Trial on Stress, Physical Touch, and Social Identity." *Comprehensive Psychoneuroendocrinology*
8: 10091.

Ferrajão, P. C., and A. Elklit. 2020. "World Assumptions and Posttraumatic Stress in a Treatment-Seeking
Sample of Survivors of Childhood Sexual Abuse: A Longitudinal Study." *Psychology of Violence*
10(5): 501–508.

Karakurt, G., and K. E. Silver. 2014. "Therapy for Sexual Abuse Survivors Using Attachment and Family
Systems Theory Orientations." *The American Journal of Family Therapy* 42(1): 79–91.

Kaye-Tzadok, A., and B. Davidson-Arad. 2016. "Posttraumatic Growth Among Women Survivors of
Childhood Sexual Abuse: Its Relation to Cognitive Strategies, Posttraumatic Symptoms, and
Resilience." *Psychological Trauma: Theory, Research, Practice, and Policy* 8(5): 550–558.

Leahy, R. L. 2019. "Introduction: Emotional Schemas and Emotional Schema Therapy." *International
Journal of Cognitive Therapy* 12(1): 1–4.

Levenkron, S., and A. Levenkron. 2007. *Stolen Tomorrows: Understanding and Treating Women's Childhood Sexual Abuse*. New York: Norton.

MacGinley, M., J. Breckenridge, and J. Mowell. 2019. "A Scoping Review of Adult Survivors' Experiences of Shame Following Sexual Abuse in Childhood." *Health and Social Care in the Community* 27: 1135–1146.

McKay, M., and P. Fanning. 1991. *Prisoners of Belief: Exposing and Changing Beliefs That Control Your Life*. Oakland, CA: New Harbinger Publications.

McKay, M., and A. West. 2016. *Emotion Efficacy Therapy: A Brief, Exposure-Based Treatment for Emotion Regulation Integrating ACT and DBT*. Oakland, CA: Context Press/New Harbinger Publications.

Neff, K. 2023. "Self-Compassion: Theory, Method, Research, and Intervention." *Annual Review of Psychology* 74: 7.1–7.26.

———. 2009. "Self-Compassion." In *Handbook of Individual Differences in Social Behavior*, edited by M. R. Leary and R. H. Hoyle. New York: Guilford Press.

Oh, V. K. S., A. Sarwar, and N. Pervez. 2022. "The Study of Mindfulness as an Intervening Factor for Enhanced Psychological Well-Being in Building the Level of Resilience." *Frontiers in Psychology* 13: 1–8.

Seltzer, L. 2008. "The Path to Unconditional Self-Acceptance: How Do You Fully Accept Yourself When You Don't Know How?" *Psychology Today*, September 10. https://www.psychologytoday.com/us/blog /evolution-the-self/200809/the-path-unconditional-self-acceptance.

Tanasugarn, A. 2022. "3 Unmet Basic Needs and Their Effects on Relationships." *Psychology Today*, December 11. https://www.psychologytoday.com/us/blog/understanding-ptsd/202212/3-unmet -basic-needs-and-their-effects-on-relationships.

Tang, Y. Y. 2017. *The Neuroscience of Mindfulness Meditation: How Our Body and Mind Work Together to Change Our Behavior*. London: Palgrave MacMillan.

Taylor, S. C., and C. Norma. 2013. "The Ties That Bind: Family Barriers for Adult Women Seeking to Report Childhood Sexual Assault in Australia." *Women's Studies International Forum* 37: 114–124.

Tull, M. T., K. S. Hahn, S. D. Evans, K. Salters-Pedneault, and K. L. Gratz. 2011. "Examining the Role of Emotional Avoidance in the Relationship Between Posttraumatic Stress Disorder Symptom Severity and Worry." *Cognitive Behaviour Therapy* 40(1): 5–14.

van der Kolk, B. A. 2014. *The Body Keeps the Score: Brain, Mind, and Body in the Healing of Trauma*. New York: Viking.

Young, J. E., J. S. Kiodko, and M. E. Welshaar. 2003. *Schema Therapy: A Practitioner's Guide*. New York: Guilford Press.

Younique Foundation. 2017. *Supporting Hope: Helping a Loved One Through Their Healing Journey*. Lehi, UT: Younique Foundation. https://youniquefoundation.org/wp-content/uploads/2016/08/Supporting-Hope -Generic.pdf.

Stacey R. Pinatelli, PsyD, received her doctorate in clinical psychology from the California School of Professional Psychology at Alliant International University in Emeryville, CA. She completed her internship in clinical psychology at VA Northern California Health Care System, East Bay. She is completing her postdoctoral fellowship at Palo Alto VA Medical Center. She has clinical experience working with a diverse population of clients, including veterans, adolescents, trauma survivors across gender identifications, and clients experiencing learning difficulties requesting a neuropsychological assessment.

Pinatelli's work with veterans and trauma survivors has provided her with a strong foundation evaluating and treating clients with simple and complex post-traumatic stress disorder (PTSD) and comorbid psychiatric difficulties, as well as experience utilizing exposure-based treatment. She was previously involved in a study that implements hybrid protocols of acceptance and commitment therapy (ACT); ACT and eye movement desensitization and reprocessing (EMDR); and ACT and written exposure therapy for PTSD symptoms, comorbid anxiety, depression, stress, psychological flexibility, state arousal and valence, values-based living, and interpersonal functioning. She is an active member of the Association for Contextual Behavioral Science (ACBS), American Psychological Association (APA), and has been an AmeriCorps Member—Corporation for National and Community Service in her past clinical services.

Foreword writer **Robyn D. Walser, PhD**, is director of TL Consultation and Psychological Services, and codirector of Bay Area Trauma Recovery Clinical Services. She has authored and coauthored several books, including *The Heart of ACT* and *Acceptance and Commitment Therapy for the Treatment of Post-Traumatic Stress Disorder and Trauma-Related Problems*.

Real change *is* possible

For more than fifty years, New Harbinger has published proven-effective self-help books and pioneering workbooks to help readers of all ages and backgrounds improve mental health and well-being, and achieve lasting personal growth. In addition, our spirituality books offer profound guidance for deepening awareness and cultivating healing, self-discovery, and fulfillment.

Founded by psychologist Matthew McKay and Patrick Fanning, New Harbinger is proud to be an independent, employee-owned company. Our books reflect our core values of integrity, innovation, commitment, sustainability, compassion, and trust. Written by leaders in the field and recommended by therapists worldwide, New Harbinger books are practical, accessible, and provide real tools for real change.

 **newharbinger**publications

MORE BOOKS from
NEW HARBINGER PUBLICATIONS

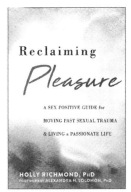

RECLAIMING PLEASURE

A Sex Positive Guide for
Moving Past Sexual Trauma
and Living a Passionate Life

978-1684038428 / US $18.95

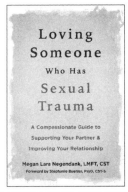

**LOVING SOMEONE WHO
HAS SEXUAL TRAUMA**

A Compassionate Guide to
Supporting Your Partner and
Improving Your Relationship

978-1648481574 / US $19.95

**THE ADVERSE
CHILDHOOD EXPERIENCES
GUIDED JOURNAL**

Neuroscience-Based Writing Practices
to Rewire Your Brain from Trauma

978-1648484155 / US $19.95

A MOMENT FOR ME

52 Simple Mindfulness Practices
to Slow Down, Relieve Stress,
and Nourish the Spirit

978-1684035182 / US $18.95

◉ REVEAL PRESS
An Imprint of New Harbinger Publications

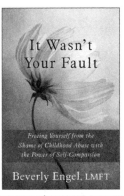

IT WASN'T YOUR FAULT

Freeing Yourself from the
Shame of Childhood Abuse with
the Power of Self-Compassion

978-1626250994 / US $21.95

**PUT YOUR
ANXIETY HERE**

A Creative Guided Journal to
Relieve Stress and Find Calm

978-1648481451 / US $18.95

Did you know there are **free tools** you can download for this book?

Free tools are things like **worksheets**, **guided meditation exercises**, and **more** that will help you get the most out of your book.

You can download free tools for this book—whether you bought or borrowed it, in any format, from any source—from the New Harbinger website. All you need is a NewHarbinger.com account. Just use the URL provided in this book to view the free tools that are available for it. Then, click on the "download" button for the free tool you want, and follow the prompts that appear to log in to your NewHarbinger.com account and download the material.

You can also save the free tools for this book to your **Free Tools Library** so you can access them again anytime, just by logging in to your account! Just look for this button on the book's free tools page.

+ Save this to my free tools library